Marx Joyce
Abbott Hardy Machiavelli Chesterton Cooper Emerson Austen
Defoe Melville Montaigne Haggard Hugo Grimm
Carroll Christie Molière Eliot
Stoker Maupassant Byron Schiller
Wilde Engels
Garnett Fitzgerald Hawthorne Smith Kafka Hall
Goethe Einstein Dostoyevsky Willis
Cotton Kipling Doyle
Baum Henry Nietzsche
Leslie Dumas Flaubert Turgenev Balzac
Stockton Vatsyayana Crane
Burroughs Verne
Curtis Tocqueville Gogol Vinci
Homer Widger Tolstoy Whitman Busch
Darwin Thoreau Twain Scott Plato Harte
Potter Freud Zola Lawrence Dickens Burton Hesse
Kant Jowett Stevenson Cervantes Voltaire
Andersen Cooke
London Descartes
Poe Aristotle Wells Irving
Hale James Hastings
Bunner Shakespeare
Richter Chambers da Benedict Alcott
Doré Dante Chekhov Shaw Wodehouse Pushkin
Swift Newton

 tredition®

tredition was established in 2006 by Sandra Latusseck and Soenke Schulz. Based in Hamburg, Germany, tredition offers publishing solutions to authors and publishing houses, combined with world-wide distribution of printed and digital book content. tredition is uniquely positioned to enable authors and publishing houses to create books on their own terms and without conventional manufacturing risks.

For more information please visit: www.tredition.com

TREDITION CLASSICS

This book is part of the TREDITION CLASSICS series. The creators of this series are united by passion for literature and driven by the intention of making all public domain books available in printed format again - worldwide. Most TREDITION CLASSICS titles have been out of print and off the bookstore shelves for decades. At tredition we believe that a great book never goes out of style and that its value is eternal. Several mostly non-profit literature projects provide content to tredition. To support their good work, tredition donates a portion of the proceeds from each sold copy. As a reader of a TREDITION CLASSICS book, you support our mission to save many of the amazing works of world literature from oblivion. See all available books at www.tredition.com.

Project Gutenberg

The content for this book has been graciously provided by Project Gutenberg. Project Gutenberg is a non-profit organization founded by Michael Hart in 1971 at the University of Illinois. The mission of Project Gutenberg is simple: To encourage the creation and distribution of eBooks. Project Gutenberg is the first and largest collection of public domain eBooks.

Australian Search Party

Charles Henry Eden

Imprint

This book is part of TREDITION CLASSICS

Author: Charles Henry Eden
Cover design: Buchgut, Berlin – Germany

Publisher: tredition GmbH, Hamburg - Germany
ISBN: 978-3-8424-5497-2

www.tredition.com
www.tredition.de

AUSTRALIAN SEARCH PARTY

BY

CHARLES HENRY EDEN

FROM
ILLUSTRATED TRAVELS:
A RECORD OF
DISCOVERY, GEOGRAPHY, AND ADVENTURE.

EDITED BY
H.W. BATES,
ASSISTANT-SECRETARY OF THE ROYAL GEOGRAPHICAL SOCIE-
TY.

AN AUSTRALIAN SEARCH PARTY — I.

BY CHARLES H. EDEN.

IN a former narrative, published in the preceding volume of the ILLUSTRATED TRAVELS, I gave an account of a terrible cyclone which visited the north-eastern coast of Queensland in the autumn of 1866, nearly destroying the small settlements of Cardwell and Townsville, and doing an infinity of damage by uprooting heavy timber, blocking up the bush roads, etc. Amongst other calamities attendant on this visitation was the loss of a small coasting schooner, named the 'Eva', bound from Cleveland to Rockingham Bay, with cargo and passengers. Only those who have visited Australia can picture to themselves the full horror of a captivity amongst the degraded blacks with whom this unexplored district abounds; and a report of white men having been seen amongst the wild tribes in the neighbourhood of the Herbert River induced the inhabitants of Cardwell to institute a search party to rescue the crew of the unhappy schooner, should they still be alive; or to gain some certain clue to their fate, should they have perished.

In my former narrative I described our exploration of the Herbert River, lying at the south end of Rockingham Channel, with its fruitless issue; and I now take up the thread of my story from that point, thinking it can hardly fail to be of interest to the reader, not only as regards the wild nature of the country traversed, but also as showing the anxiety manifested by the inhabitants of these remote districts to clear up the fate of their unhappy brethren. I may also here mention, for the information of such of my readers as may not have read the preceding portions of the narrative, that Cardwell is the name of a small township situated on the shores of Rockingham Bay; and that Townsville is a settlement some hundred miles further south, known also as Cleveland Bay.

HOW WE EXPLORED GOULD AND GARDEN ISLANDS.

We were all much pleased at a piece of intelligence brought up by the 'Daylight', to the effect that a party of volunteers had been assembled at Cleveland Bay, and intended coming up in a small steamer to the south end of Hinchinbrook, to assist in the search for the missing crew. As it would be of the utmost importance that both parties should co-operate, I sent my boat down to the mouth of the channel, with a note to the leader of the expedition announcing our intention of landing on the north end of the island and working towards the centre; and requesting them to scour their end, and then push northward, when we should most probably meet in the middle of the island. The boat had orders to wait at the bar until the arrival of the steamer, and then to return with all speed. In the meanwhile, the 'Daylight' was discharging her cargo, and we were making preparations for what we well knew would prove a most arduous undertaking; the sequel will show that we did not overrate the difficulties before us.

At the risk of being tedious, I must explain to the reader some of the peculiarities of Hinchinbrook Island. Its length is a little short of forty miles, and its shape a rude triangle, the apex of which is at the south, and the north side forming the southern portion of Rockingham Bay. Now this north side is by no means straight, but is curved out into two or three bays of considerable extent, and in one of them stand two islands named Gould and Garden Islands. The latter of these was our favourite resort for picnics, for the dense foliage afforded good shade, and, when the tide was low, we were enabled to gather most delicious oysters from some detached rocks. Gould Island is considerably larger; but, rising in a pyramid from the sea, and being covered with loose boulders, it was most tedious climbing. From the township we could, with our glasses, see canoes constantly passing and repassing between these two islands; and as the 'Daylight' had a particularly heavy cargo this trip, and would not be clear for the next two days, we made up our minds to search the islands, and drive the blacks on to Hinchinbrook, so that one of our parties must stumble across them when we swept it. This may seem to the reader unnecessary trouble, but most of our party were conversant with the habits of the blacks and their limited method of reasoning; and we judged it probable that the Herbert River gins would have at once acquainted the Hinchinbrook blacks with our unceremonious visit, and warned them that we should probably soon look them up also. Now on the receipt of this unwelcome intelligence, the first thing that would strike the blacks would be the facilities for concealment afforded by Gould or Garden Islands, more particularly had they any captives; and they would say to themselves that we should certainly overlook these two out-of-the-way little spots; and when we were busy on Hinchinbrook, they could easily paddle themselves and their prisoners to some of the more distant chain of islands, where they could lie by until all fear of pursuit was past. Such was the opinion both of the troopers and of the experienced bushmen; and as we were fully resolved to leave them no loophole for escape, we jumped into our boat and pulled gently over to Garden Island.

It was about seven o'clock in the morning when we started, six strong—four whites, and Cato, and Ferdinand—well armed, and with a good supply of provisions. The sun was already very hot, and the water smooth as glass, save where the prow of the boat broke the still surface into a tiny ripple, which continued plainly visible half a mile astern. I find it difficult to bring before the reader the thousand curious objects that met us on our way. The sullen crocodile basking in the sun, sank noiselessly; a splash would be heard, and a four feet albicore would fling himself madly into the air, striving vainly to elude the ominous black triangle that cut the water like a knife close in his rear. Small chance for the poor fugitive, with the ravenous shark following silent and inexorable. We lay on our oars and watched the result. The hunted fish doubles, springs aloft, and dives down, but all in vain; the black fin is not to be thrown off, double as he may. Anon the springs become more feeble, the pursuer's tail partly appears as he pushes forward with redoubled vigour, a faint splash is heard, the waters curl into an eddy, and the monster sinks noiselessly to enjoy his breakfast in the cooler depths beneath. And now we come to a sand bank running out some miles or so into the bay, and on which the water is less than three fathoms. Here the surface is broken by huge black objects, coming clumsily to the top, shooting out a jet of spray, and again disappearing. We let the boat glide gently along until she rests motionless above the bank, and stooping over the side with our faces close to the water, and sheltered by our hands, we can peer down into the placid depths, and see the huge animals grazing on the submarine vegetation with which their favourite feeding-place is thickly overgrown. But what animal is he talking about? the reader will ask. It is the dugong ('Halicore Australis'), or sea-cow, from whence is extracted an oil equal to the cod-liver as regards its medicinal qualities, and far superior to it in one great essential, for instead of a nauseous disagreeable flavour, it tastes quite pleasantly. It frequents the whole of the north-eastern coast of Australia, and when the qualities of the oil first became known, it was eagerly sought after by invalids who could not overcome their repugnance to the cod-liver nastiness. The fishermen, however, spoilt their own market, for greed induced them to adulterate the new medicine with shark oil, and all kinds of other abominations, so that the faculty were never quite certain what they were pouring down the throats of their unhappy patients. Thus the oil lost its good name, though I am convinced from personal observation that fresh, pure dugong is quite equal, if not superior, in nourishing qualities to cod-liver oil, and do not doubt that a time will come when it will enter largely into the Pharmacopoeia. The animal itself is so peculiar, that a brief description of it may not be here amiss. Its favourite haunts are bays into which streams empty themselves, and where the water is from two to five fathoms in depth, feeding on the 'Algae' of the submerged banks, for which purpose the upper lip is very large, thick, and as it turns down suddenly at right angles with the head, it much resembles an elephant's trunk shorn off at the mouth. Its length averages from eight to fourteen feet; there is no dorsal fin, and the tail is horizontal; colour blue, and white beneath. Its means of propulsion are two paddles, with which it also crawls along the bottom, and beneath which are situated the udders, with teats exactly like a cow's. Its flesh is far from bad, resembling lean beef in appearance, though hardly so good to the taste, and the skin can be manufactured into gelatine. I have often wondered that this most useful animal was not oftener captured. A fishing establishment with a good boat, a trained crew, and proper appliances for extracting the oil, could not fail to return a large profit to the proprietors, and every now and then they could kill a whale, one or more of which could be frequently seen disporting themselves in the waters of the bay.

[Illustration—BAY ON HINCHINBROOK ISLAND, WITH NATIVES.]

By ten o'clock we had reached Garden Island, and beached the boat on a long sandy spit that stretched into the sea. Leaving one man as boat-keeper, we spread ourselves into line, and regularly beat the little island from end to end, but without finding a single black; we could, however, see their smoke-signals arising from Gould Island, and observed several heavily-laden canoes making the best of their way towards Hinchinbrook. Our search having been unsuccessful, we hurried down to the boat, with the intention of cutting the fugitives off, but found to our disgust that the tide had fallen so low during our absence that our united strength was insufficient to move the boat, so we were perforce compelled to remain until the return of the water. This did not in reality so much signify, indeed, some of the party were rather averse to our plan of intercepting the canoes, arguing that if closely pressed, the blacks might make an end of their captives. However this might be, there was no help for it, we were stuck fast until the afternoon, so had to summon such philosophy as we possessed, and while away the time as best we could. The boat's sail, spread under the shade of a tree, kept the intense heat a little at bay until after dinner, and this most essential part of the day's programme have been done ample justice to, and the pipes lighted and smoked out, we wandered about the long space left bare by the tide, amusing ourselves by collecting oysters, cowrie shells, and periwinkles.

The way we captured the two latter was by turning over the rocks, to the under sides of which we found them adhering in great numbers, sticking on like snails to a garden wall. Some of the cowries were very beautiful, particularly those of a deep brown colour approaching to black. This kind, however, were rather rare, and the lucky finder of a large one excited some envy. These beautiful little shells are of all sizes, from half an inch to two inches in length. When the stone is first turned over, the fish is almost out of its home, and the bright colour of the shell is hidden by a fleshy integument, but a few seconds suffice for it to withdraw within doors, and then the mottled pattern is seen in its full beauty. The best way to get the shell without injury to its gloss, is to keep the fish alive in a bucket of salt water, until you reach home, and then to dig a hole a couple of feet deep, and bury them. In a month or so, they may be taken up, and will be found quite clean, free from smell, and as bright in hue as during life. I have tried boiling them, heaping them in the sun, and various other methods, but this is undoubtedly the best.

[Illustration—SATIN BOWER-BIRDS]

Should it ever fall to the lot of any of my readers to have to cook periwinkles—and there are many worse things, when you are certain of their freshness—let them remember that they should be boiled in 'salt water'. This is to give them toughness; if fresh water is used, however expert the operator may be with his pin, he will fail to extract more than a moiety of the curly delicacy. These little facts, though extraneous to our subject, are always worth knowing.

At one end of Garden Island, and distant from it about 200 yards, stands a very singular rock, of a whitish hue, and when struck at a certain angle by the sun, so much resembling the canvas of a vessel, that it was named the "Sail Rock." At low tide this could be reached by wading, the water being little more than knee-deep. Its base was literally covered with oysters of the finest quality. The mere task of getting there was one of considerable difficulty, for the rock was as slippery as glass, and whenever you got a fall—which happened on an average every five minutes—bleeding hands and jagged knees bore testimony to a couch of growing bivalves being anything but as soft as a feather bed; also the oysters cling so fast that they might be taken for component parts of the rock, and only a cold chisel and mallet will induce them to relinquish their firm embrace. Three or four of the party had ventured out, and we had secured a large sackful, after which we all retired to the tent, except one of our number, who, having a lady-love in Cardwell with an inordinate affection for shell-fish, lingered to fill a haversack for his 'inamorata'. We were comfortably smoking our pipes and watching with satisfaction the tide rising higher and higher, when a faint "coo-eh" from the direction of the rock reached us, followed by another and another and another, each one more shrill than the last.

"By Jove, Wordsworth's in some trouble!" exclaimed one of our party, and, snatching up our carbines, we hurried to the end of the island at which stood the Sail Rock. The tide had now risen considerably, and the water between the rock and ourselves was over four feet deep, and increasing in depth each moment. We saw poor Wordsworth clinging on to the slippery wall, as high up as the smooth mass afforded hand-hold.

"Come along, old fellow!" we shouted; "it's not up to your neck yet."

"He turned his head over his shoulder—even at the distance we were, its pallor was quite visible—and slowly and cautiously releasing one hand, he pointed to the water between himself and the island.

"By Jove!" cried the pilot, "he's bailed up by a shark, look at his sprit-sail!" and following his finger we saw an enormous black fin sailing gently to and fro, as regularly and methodically as a veteran sentry paces the limits of his post.

"Stick tight, old man! we'll bring the boat," and leaving the pilot to keep up a fusillade at the monster with the carbines, we darted back. I shall never forget the efforts we made to launch the boat, but she was immovable, and every moment the tide was rising, the little ripples expending themselves in bubbly foam against the thirsty sand. We strained, we tugged, we prised with levers, but unavailingly, the boat seemed as if she had taken root there and would not budge an inch. A happy thought struck me all of a sudden, as a reminiscence of a similar case that I had seen in years gone by came back in full vigour.

"Give me a tomahawk," I said.

One was produced in a minute from under the stern-sheets. Meanwhile I had got out a couple of the oars.

"Now, Jim, you're the best axeman, off with them here!"

Half a dozen strokes to each, and the blades were severed from the looms.

"Now boys, lay aft and lift her stern."

It was done, and one of the oars placed under as a roller.

"Now, launch together."

"Heave with a will."

"She's moving!"

"Again so. Keep her going."

"Hurrah!" and a loud cheer broke forth, as, through the medium of the friendly rollers, the heavy boat trundled into the water.

The pull was long, at least it seemed to us long, for we had to round the sandy spit before we could head towards the rock, and nearly got on shore in trying to make too close a shave. We could hear the crack of the pilot's carbine every few minutes, borne down to us by the freshening breeze, and the agonising "coo-ehs" of poor Wordsworth, whose ankles were already hidden by the advancing waters; added to this, we had only two oars, and the wind, now pretty strong, was dead in our teeth. I was steering, and Jim was standing up in the bows with his carbine for a shot, if the shark offered such an opportunity. As we neared the rock we could distinctly see the black fin within six feet of the narrow ledge on which the poor fellow was standing, and only when we approached to within a couple of boats' lengths, did the ferocious brute sail sullenly out to sea, pursued by a harmless bullet from Jim's rifle. Poor Wordsworth dropped into the boat fainting from terror, exhaustion, and loss of blood, for, although he was unconscious of it all the time, in his convulsive grip, the sharp oyster-shells had cut his hands to the very bone. A good glass of grog and some hot tea—the bushman's infallible remedy—soon brought him round, but the scars on his hands and knees will accompany him to his grave. He afterwards described the glances that the shark threw at him as perfectly diabolical, and confessed that he it not been for the cheery hails of the pilot, he should most certainly have relinquished his hold, and met with a death too horrible to contemplate.

It was now about three o'clock in the afternoon, and the boat being launched, we resolved to reach Gould Island before dark. The tent was soon struck, the provisions stowed away, the priming of the carbines looked to afresh, and in a few minutes we were sweeping across the small belt of water that separated the two islands. We approached the shore with caution, for, as I mentioned before, the sides of Gould Island are everywhere very steep, and hostile blacks, by simply dislodging some of the loose masses of rock, could easily have smashed the boat and its crew to pieces without exposing themselves to the slightest danger. Noiselessly, and with every faculty painfully alert, we closed the land, sprang on to the rocks, and at once set about the tedious task of breasting the hill. Hill climbing, under the vertical sun of North Australia, is by no means an enjoyable undertaking, more particularly when the loose shale and rock gives way at every stride, bringing down an avalanche of rubbish on the heads of the rearmost of the party. Encumbered with our carbines, we made but slow progress, and it was nearly six o'clock before we attained the summit, from whence we saw several canoes making their way with full speed towards Hinchinbrook.

"So far then, so good," we said; "we have made certain that none of the rascals are lurking about the two islands, and we are sure to get them now, when we sweep Hinchinbrook."

We had now done everything that was possible until the 'Daylight' had finished unloading, and so spread ourselves out about the island to see if the blacks had left any of their curious implements behind them. We were in no hurry to get back to the township, so purposed having supper where we were, and pulling back in the cool of the evening, by the light of the moon, which was just then in full glory. We found plenty of traces of the blacks, the embers of their fires even still glowing, but they had carried off everything with them, and no trophies crowned our search of Gould Island; and yet I am wrong, for I got one memento, which I have by me still, and which is so curious to lovers of natural history that I am tempted to describe it. In rummaging about, I came to a place strewed with old bones, shells, parrots' feathers, etc., close to which stood a platform of interwoven sticks. I was terribly puzzled at first to account for the presence of this miniature rag and bone depot, and my astonishment culminated when Ferdinand informed me that—

"Bird been make it that fellow; plenty d—d thief that fellow, steal like it pipe, like it anything."

It then flashed across me that I had fallen in with the "run" of the bower-bird, of which I had so often heard, and had so often sought for without success.

The satin bower-bird ('Ptilonorhynchus holosericus') belongs to the family of starlings, and though tolerably common in New South Wales, is but a rare visitor to the hotter climate of Northern Queensland. The plumage of the adult male is of a glossy satin-like purple, appearing almost black, whilst the females and the young are all of an olive-greenish colour. The peculiarity for which this bird is generally known, is its habit of constructing a sort of arbour of dry twigs, to act as a playground. These bowers are usually made in some secluded place in the bush—not infrequently under the shady boughs of a large tree—and vary considerably in size, according to the number of birds resorting to them, for they seem to be joint-stock affairs, and are not limited to one pair. The bower itself is somewhat difficult to describe, and a better idea can be formed from the engraving, or by visiting the British Museum, where several are shown, than I can ever hope to set before the reader in words. A number of sticks, most artistically woven together, form the base, from the centre of which the walls of the structure arise. These walls are made of lighter twigs, and considerable pains must be taken in their selection, for they all have an inward curve, which in some "runs" cause the sides almost to meet at the top. The degree of fore-thought that these self-taught architects possess is strikingly exemplified in the fact that, whilst building the walls, any forks or inequalities are turned 'outwards', so as to offer no impediment to their free passage when skylarking (if it is not an Irishism, using such an expression with regard to a starling) and chasing each other through and through the bower, to which innocent recreations, according to the testimony of Messrs. Cato and Ferdinand, they devote the major part of their time. Their love of finery and gaudy colours is also most remarkable. Interwoven amongst the twigs of which the bower is composed, and scattered about the ground in its vicinity, are found bleached bones, broken oyster, snail, and cowrie shells, and not unfrequently, in the more civilised districts, pieces of coloured rag, and fragments of ribbon pilfered from some neighbouring station, for, in search of attractive objects to decorate his playground, the bower-bird entirely ignores the eighth commandment, and, I fear, justifies the somewhat strong expression of "d—d thief" which Ferdinand bestowed on him. Indeed, so well are his filching propensities known to the natives, that they make a practice of searching the runs whenever any small article of value is missing, and often succeed in recovering the lost object.

I find that I have been using the pronoun 'he' hitherto, whilst describing this insatiable love of finery, but on reflection I cannot but think that I am utterly wrong, and that when more is known of the domestic arrangements of the bower-bird, it will be found that the lady alone is responsible for this meretricious taste, and that the poor 'he', whom I have so unblushingly accused, is in reality gathering berries and fruit for the little ones, guiltless of the slightest inclination towards picking and stealing.

These birds live and thrive in confinement, and busy themselves immensely in the construction of runs, but they never multiply whilst captive. Indeed, the place and manner of their breeding is as yet a mystery, for, so skilful are they in concealment, that even the lynx-eyed blacks have failed to discover their next.

We found the descent to the boat incomparably preferable to the tedious climb of two hours previous, and, thanks to the promise of a "nobbler of rum each," Cato and Ferdinand transported my precious "run" in safety to the stern-sheets; the sun having then sunk in crimson beauty behind the coast-range, and the breeze having fallen to the faintest whisper, we shoved off, and pulled leisurely over the calm bay to Cardwell, arriving about ten o'clock, to hear the welcome news that the 'Daylight' would be ready for us on the following afternoon.

HOW WE EXPLORED HINCHINBROOK ISLAND.

The sun was just showing above the distant sea-line, and the bay was lying motionless as a mirror, with a rosy hue thrown across its placid surface, when I awoke on the following morning, stiff from the clamber of the preceding day. The short half-hour before the rays of the sun have attained an unpleasant fierceness is most enjoyable in Australia, particularly in a wild region such as Cardwell, where birds, beasts, and fishes pursue their daily avocations, heedless of the presence of man. My house was situated at the extreme north end of the township, and far apart from the nearest dwelling—so much so, in fact, that it was only by a stretch of the imagination that I could say I was included within the village boundary. On the side farthest from the settlement lay the virgin bush, whilst outside the garden at the back, all was wild and rude as Nature had left it, except a small clearing I had made for the growth of maize, sweet potatoes, etc. Now this clearing had many enemies, and of many species, ranging from feathered and furred to biped. The cockatoos came down in such clouds as almost to whiten the ground, and made short work of the maize; the bandicoots and the township pigs dug up and devoured the sweet potatoes, just as they were becoming large enough for use—commend me to your half-starved pig to find out in a moment where the juiciest and finest esculent lies buried—and the chattering little opossums stripped the peach-trees of their wealth, in which labour of love they were eagerly assisted by the flying-foxes during the night, whilst any that had escaped these nocturnal depredators became the spoil of two or three idle boys, who loafed about all day, seeking mischief, and, as always happens, succeeding in finding it, even in this sequestered region. From this it will be seen that my efforts in the direction of husbandry were attended with some difficulty, and, despite a real liking for the animal world, I had imbibed a holy hatred of that particular section of its society which insisted on devouring my substance under my very nose, only retreating to the nearest tree until my back was turned, and then resuming operations with unblushing effrontery. By way of a mild vengeance, I had got into the habit of coming out every morning directly I awoke, with my gun, and easing off both barrels amongst the cockatoos, wallabies, or whatever particular class of robbers happened to be afield at the moment—a practice which served as a safety-valve for my injured feelings, whilst at the same time it provided me with a cockatoo pie, or a good bowl of kangaroo-tail soup.

Once, in my indignation at finding my palings broken down, and some sugar-cane, that I had been most carefully rearing, rooted up and destroyed, while the author of the mischief, a huge sow, innocent of the restraining ring (I would have hung the ring of the 'Devastation's' best bower-anchor to her snout, had I been allowed to follow out my wishes), stood gloating over the havoc she had caused. Then, in my wrath, I had hastily loaded a carbine with a handful of salt, and prematurely converted a portion of my enemy's flank into bacon; but even this just act of retribution was not to be accomplished without further loss to myself, for on receipt of my hint to move on, her sowship dashed straight ahead, and brought down a whole panel of my fence about her ears, owing to which the village cows, which I had often observed throwing longing glances over the paling at my bananas, doubtless apprised of their opportunity by the evil-minded and malicious sow, took a mean advantage of the weakness of my defences, and on the same night devoured everything in the garden that they thought worthy of their attention.

Though I had now become hardened to the many injuries thus heaped upon me, and had almost discontinued all attempts at cultivation, I still retained the habit of stepping out into the verandah every morning with my gun, but more with an eye to the pot than for any other reason.

Beautiful as the scene always was, it struck me that day as being of unusual splendour. The tall gum-trees, with their naked stems, and curious hanging leaves that exasperate the heated traveller by throwing the scantiest of shadows, glistened dew-beaded in the rising sun. The laughing jackass, perched upon a bare limb, was awaking the forest echoes with his insane fits of laughter, alternating from a good-humoured chuckle to the frenzied ravings of a despairing maniac. Suddenly ceasing, he would dart down upon some hapless lizard, too early astir for its own safety, and, with his writhing prey in his bill, would fly to some other branch, and after swallowing his captive, burst forth into a yell of self-gratulation even-more fiendish than before. The delicate little "paddy melon," a small species of kangaroo, turned his gracefully-formed little head, beautiful as a fawn's, and, startled at the strange figure in the verandah, stood hesitatingly for a few seconds, and then, bending forward, bounded into the scrub, the noise caused by the flapping of its tail being audible long after the little animal itself was lost to sight. The white cockatoos, alarmed by the outcry of the sentry — for, like the English rooks, they always tell off some of their number to keep a look-out — who with sulphur-coloured crest, erect and outstretched neck, kept up a constant cry of warning, rose from the maize patch, the spotless white of their plumage glancing in the sun, and forming a beautiful contrast to the pale straw-colour of the under portion of their extended pinions. With discordant screams they circle about, as if a little undetermined, and then perch upon the topmost branches of the tallest trees, where they screech, flap their wings, and engage in a series of either imaginary combats, or affectionate caresses, until, the coast being clear, they are again enabled to continue their repast.

A curious and indescribable wailing cry is heard in the air, singularly depressing in its effect, and a string of some dozen black cockatoos flit from tree to tree, the brilliant scarlet band on the tail of the male flashing as he alternately expands and contracts it, to keep his balance whilst extracting the sweets from the flowers of the 'Eucalypti'. Few things present so great a contrast as the cries of these two birds — of the same family, and so alike in everything but colour — and yet both are disagreeable: that of the white variety from its piercing harshness, and that of the black from an indefinable sensation of the approach of coming evil it carries with it — at least, such is the effect it always has upon me. On strolling to the paling and looking into the clearing — for although my gun is in my hand, it is loaded with ball cartridge, and I do not fire — the nimble little bandicoot scuttled away towards his hollow log, looking so uncommonly like a well-fattened rat, that I mentally wonder how I could ever have had the courage to eat one, and a flight of rainbow-hued Blue Mountain parrots, who have held their ground to the last, whirr up with a prodigious flapping of wings, and, alighting on a gum-tree, can be seen hanging about the blossoms, head downwards, sucking out the honey with their uncouth beaks and awkward little tongues, which seem but badly adapted to such a delicate task. But I find I am digressing terribly, and the gloomy winter days of England, which make the recollection of a bright tropical morning so agreeable a task to contemplate, must be my excuse.

After breakfast, I hurried down to the beach to see if Tom Frewin, the skipper of the little cutter, 'Daylight', would be likely to keep his promise, and have the vessel ready to start by noon. I found him busily engaged with his not over-numerous crew — for it consisted only of a man and a boy, besides himself, though Mrs. Tom, who also lived in the tiny craft, ought to be counted as no inconsiderable addition to the vessel's complement, for she did the cooking, and on occasions could take the tiller and steer as cunningly as the gallant Tom himself. I found him hard at work hurrying the cargo over the side, assisted by the townspeople, who all showed the greatest anxiety that no time should be lost in setting out for the relief of the shipwrecked men. Everything thus pointing to the probability of our getting away that afternoon, the provision question had to be next considered, for the party would be numerous, and the exact time our expedition would take could scarcely be correctly estimated. We knew Government would refund us for any reasonable outlay, and so determined our search should not be cut short by any scarcity of food, and our fears of overshooting the mark and laying in more than we could consume, were allayed by Mr. McB—, the store-keeper who generously offered to supply us, and to take back, without charge, anything that remained at the expiration of the trip. All difficulties being thus disposed of, we were left at liberty to make our own private arrangements, until one o'clock, by which time the 'Daylight' would have laid in her water, etc., and be ready to start.

But I must now say something of the party itself, which we were compelled to limit to ten men, inclusive of the native police. These consisted of the pilot and his crew of two men, Mr. Dunmore, the officer in command of the police, with the two troopers, Ferdinand and Cato, three volunteers, and myself. Where all were anxious and willing to aid in the good task, it would have been invidious to select, and the volunteers drew lots from a bag in which all were blanks but three, the gainers of these lucky numbers becoming members of the party.

One other addition we had, and right yeoman's service she did, for it was a 'she', reader as the sequel will prove. About eighteen months before, the troopers had visited Hinchinbrook Island, to recover stolen property, and in one of the native camps had found an exceedingly pretty gin of some fourteen summers. The personal charms of this coy nymph of the forest had proved too much for the susceptible heart of Ferdinand, who, regarding her as his lawful prize, had borne her, irate and struggling, to the boat, from whence she was in due course transported to the police camp (mounted on the pommel of the saddle in front of the adventurous swain), where, in a very short time she became perfectly at home, and under the name of Lizzie, made Ferdinand a remarkably pleasant wife.

Certainly the blacks are a curious race, the like of which was never before seen under the sun. For two days after Lizzie's arrival in camp, she refused to speak or eat; for the next two days she ate everything she could lay her hands on, but still kept an unbroken silence; and for another two days, whenever she was not eating, she "yabbered" so much and so fast that the other gins looked on aghast, unable to get a word in edgewise, so continuous was the flow of Hinchinbrook vituperation. On the seventh day, as if by magic, she brought her tirade to a close, went down to the creek with the other gins to fetch water, cooked her husband's supper, appeared perfectly reconciled to her change of life, and henceforth, from her sharpness, the aptitude with which she picked up the broken English in which the officers communicate with the troopers, and her great knowledge of the surrounding country, she became a most useful acquisition to the camp, and Dunmore used frequently to say that Lizzie was worth three extra troopers. One of the most extraordinary things about her—and she was not unique, for all the Australian blacks are alike constituted in this respect—was the facility with which she seemed to rupture all the natural ties of kinship and affection. Her own tribe—her father, mother, sisters, all were apparently wiped from her mind as completely as writing is removed from a slate by a sponge; or, if ever remembered, it was never with any mark of regret.

AN AUSTRALIAN SEARCH PARTY — II.

BY CHARLES H. EDEN.

BETWEEN one and two o'clock, the report of a little swivel gun, with which the taffrail of the 'Daylight' was armed, echoed over the bay, and announced to the party that all was in readiness. In a very few minutes we were all mustered on the beach, looking, I must confess, remarkably like brigands, in our slouching and high-crowned Californian hats, coatless, and with shirt-sleeves either tucked up or cut off above the elbow, which, with the carbine that each man carried in his hand, and the revolvers, knives, etc., stuck into the waist-belts, made our 'tout ensemble' such, that I am convinced no honest citizen, with a plethoric purse, who saw us thus for the first time, would have felt quite at his ease in our company. With a ringing cheer from the townspeople assembled on the beach, under the shade of the big trees, we shoved off, and, manned by willing hands, the cable rattled in, in a fashion that must have astonished the old windlass, accustomed to the leisurely proceedings that usually obtained on board the 'Daylight'. The sail was soon clapped on, the little vessel heeled over to the sea-breeze now setting in pretty stiffly, and ten minutes after quitting the shore we were down in the hold, the captain and his lady occupying the cabin. Making our preparations for the night, which consisted, I may mention, mainly of spreading out our blankets, whilst the 'Daylight', with the Government whale-boat towing astern, was beating up against the adverse wind for the north end of Hinchinbrook, where we purposed anchoring for the night, and commencing our search on the following morning.

What with a contrary wind and tide, it was not until past ten o'clock that we glided into the little bay, and, shortening sail as noiselessly as possible, let down the anchor by hand to avoid the rattling of the chain through the hawsehole, which, in the stillness of the night, would have certainly reached the keen ears of the blacks, were there any in the neighbourhood, and caused them to shift their quarters. The little inlet or creek in which we now found ourselves, was entirely new to us, and we were indebted to Lizzie for the discovery of such a quiet retreat. With straining eyes, our novel pilotess stood at the heel of the bowsprit, extending an arm in the direction she wished the vessel to go, and, her task completed, she wrapped her blanket round her active little body, scarcely shrouded in the striped twill shirt that constituted her sole attire, and, sinking down in the waterways under the lee of the gunwale, was soon sound asleep—a sensible proceeding, which, as soon as everything was secured, we hastened to imitate.

We had arranged our plans for the morrow in the following manner. Before dawn, the whale-boat was to land all the party, including Lizzie, with the exception of the pilot and his two men. He was to return to the 'Daylight' after having put us ashore, and, getting under weigh as soon as the wind was strong enough, was to take her round to a small inlet on the island, some distance down Rockingham Channel, and there await either our arrival or further instructions. Our expedition was to join him there in two or three days at the farthest, perhaps sooner; but, whatever happened, he was to remain with the cutter at the rendezvous, and on no account, nor under any inducement, was he to quit until he either saw or heard from us, however long the time might be. During the daytime the whale-boat was to be kept hauled up alongside the cutter, with the carbines belonging to the crew loaded and triced up under the thwarts, ready for immediate service, and a bright look-out was to be kept on the channel, in both directions. If the natives attempted the smallest communication with the mainland, the whale-boat was to give chase immediately, and either intercept and capture the canoes, or compel them to return to Hinchinbrook Island.

Such was the rough plan we sketched out for the guidance of the 'Daylight'. With regard to ourselves, we could make no standing rule, for the country was comparatively unknown to us, and we must, Micawber-like, trust to something turning up and, in the pursuit of this happy event, must follow whithersoever fortune and Miss Lizzie thought fit to lead us.

At least an hour before dawn we were astir, and swallowing the scalding tea that the man on watch had prepared: this done, and a snack of damper and cold meat eaten, we got quietly into the boat and were pulled ashore. Until daylight, we were unable to make our way, for paths there were none, and the ground was dangerous from the quantity of stones, etc., so we were compelled to sit down quietly and smoke our pipes until we could see to pick our way. In the tropics there is but little dawn; the sun springs up without heralding his approach by a lengthened gradation from darkness to night, as obtains in more temperate climes, and but little patience was requisite to enable us to commence our search. As many of our readers are doubtless aware that in Australia no journey is ever undertaken on foot; that the real bushman would think himself sunk to the depths of abject poverty, if he had not at least 'one' horse of his own; and that a man will wander about for a couple of hours looking for a horse to carry him half a mile, when he might have gone to his destination and back half a dozen times, in the interval wasted in searching for his steed. Knowing this, they will doubtless wonder why we did not bring our mounts with us, and perform the journey comfortably, in place of the tedious method we now adopted. It must not for a moment be imagined that the great assistance horses would have afforded us had not been duly weighted and considered, and our reasons for leaving them behind were as follows:—From the little we knew of Hinchinbrook, and from the description Lizzie gave of the country, they would have been rather in our way than otherwise. The whole island is a mass of lofty volcanic mountains; and the passes through the gorges so strewn with huge boulders, debris, and shale, that we should have been compelled to lead our nags, and thus they would have only proved an encumbrance. This was one reason, and apparently a very good one, but I doubt if it would have had much effect upon our party, who could hardly contemplate any undertaking without the agency of horseflesh, had not a more cogent argument been forthcoming, to which they were compelled to give in their adherence.

"The 'Daylight' is quite big enough to carry them all, for such a short distance, if they're properly stowed," said Jack Clark, the roughrider, who was a zealous advocate for the conveyance of his pet quadrupeds.

"Of course she can," said another; "and we shall get the work over as quickly again."

"How will you land them?" I ventured to suggest; "for the cutter can never go near enough to the shore to walk them out."

"She can't get within a quarter of a mile," said the pilot; for at this time none of us knew of the little inlet, into which Lizzie so deftly guided us.

"Pitch them overboard, of course," cried Jack; "they'll pretty soon make for the land; and I'll send my mare Gossamer first; she'll give them a lead, I'll bet. Cunning old devil!"

The impetuosity of Jack was fast gaining converts, when Cato pulled Dunmore quietly by the sleeve, and said—

"Marmy, baal you take 'em yarroman like 'it Hinchinbrook; my word, plenty of alligator sit down along of water. He been parter that fellow like 'it damper."

"By Jove! Cato's right," said Dunmore; "we forget about the alligators and sharks. I won't let the boys take their horses, and shall not take my own. I lost one horse from an alligator last year, on the Pioneer River, and Government wanted to make me pay for it, and I'll take care I don't risk losing 'three'. Bring Gossamer, if you like, Clark, but, take my word for it, you'll never see her again."

This unexpected contingency; the prophesied fate of Gossamer, which was as the apple of Jack's eye; and the point-blank and sensible refusal of Dunmore to hazard the Government horses, completely turned the tables. After a little inward grumbling, Jack consoled himself, saying—

"Well, at all events, I can 'think' of riding!"

And thus it came to pass that we landed on Hinchinbrook, with no means of locomotion beyond those with which nature had endowed us.

And now, headed by Lizzie, and walking in single file and in silence, we struck out for the interior of the island. The path—if path it could be called, for it consisted only of a dim track beaten by the naked feet of the blacks—wound in and out among the long grass, which, as we approached the foot of the mountain range, became exchanged for boulders and loose shale, which rendered walking most tedious, and played the very mischief with our boots. Here even this track seemed, to our eyes, to die out; but Lizzie led the way confidently, and evidently with a thorough knowledge of what she was about. We had now been walking for more than three hours, and had apparently only got half way up a kind of gorge in the mountains, which seemed to become gradually narrower and narrower, and from all appearances afforded every prospect of terminating in a 'cul-de-sac'. A watercourse must at some period have run down this ravine, for the boulders were rounded; but it was now quite dry. As the sides of the mountains drew nearer, our path led along this watercourse, and the walking became dreadfully fatiguing. The boulders were sometimes so close as to render walking between impossible, and then it became necessary to clamber over them, which, loaded as we were, was very painful. If, on the other hand, we attempted to journey on the 'top' of the boulders, they were not only of unequal heights, but sometimes so wide apart, that a good spring was requisite to get from one to the other. Lizzie was the only one of the party who appeared thoroughly at home; her light figure bounded from rock to rock with the greatest ease and rapidity. Even Cato and Ferdinand, barefooted as they were, seemed to be a long way from enjoying themselves, and for us wretched Europeans, with our thick boots, that obtained scarcely any foothold, we slipped about from the rounded shoulders of the rocks, in a way that was anything but pleasant.

Thus we scrambled along for another hour, at the expiration of which we could only see a blank wall of mountain before us, up which it would have been both impossible and useless to climb. Wondering where the deuce Lizzie was leading us, we blundered along until we arrived at the base of the perpendicular cliff, and saw that by some convulsion of nature the ravine now branched off at a right angle to the left, and gradually widened out into a beautiful and gently declining stretch of country, perfectly shut in by hills, and into which a pretty little bay extended, with several canoes on its placid surface. We were distant from the beach about three miles, and could see clearly the smoke of several fires; while with binocular glasses we could make out the figures of the blacks fishing, and of the piccaninnies and gins romping in the sand.

Lizzie was a sight to see, as she pointed triumphantly to the unconscious savages, and, trembling with eagerness, tapped the butt of Dunmore's carbine, as she whispered—

"Those fellow sit down there, brother belonging to me, plenty you shoot 'em, Marmy."

"You take us close up along of those fellow, Lizzie?" said Dunmore.

"Your Marmy, plenty close, you been shoot 'em all mine think," replied our amiable little guide, who, enjoining the strictest silence, at once put herself in motion, bidding us, by a sign, to follow her.

For more than an hour and a half we crept cautiously along, sometimes crawling on all fours where the country was open, and frequently stopping, while Lizzie went noiselessly forward and reconnoitred, before beckoning to us to advance again. The direction in which she led us lay at the base of the hills, which on one side bounded the little plain and its bay, and though we could form but a crude idea of where we were going, owing to the thickness of the undergrowth, yet it was sufficiently evident that the young lady was one of nature's tacticians, and meditated a flank blow at her unfortunate relatives. Proceeding, we came at last within a stone's throw of the beach, and could hear the mimic waves rolling on the sand, at no great distance, on our right hand. Lizzie now pointed to a small belt of vine shrub that lay in front of us, and indicated that immediately outside it were the 'gunyahs', or huts; and, "plenty you shoot," she added showing her white teeth as she grinned with glee at the thoughts of the cheerful surprise she had prepared for her old companions. We were not thoroughly on the 'qui vive', for we thought this unknown bay would be the very spot in which the blacks were likely to seclude any prisoners from the 'Eva', and accordingly willingly followed the lithe figure of our little guide, as she wound her way through the tangled brake, like a black snake, and with a facility that we in vain attempted to imitate. The troopers—who had reduced their clothing to a minimum, for their sole vestment consisted of a forage-cap and cartridge-belt—wound along as noiselessly as Lizzie; but we poor whites—with our flannel shirts and other complicated paraphernalia that custom would not permit us to dispense with in the matter-of-fact way they were laid aside by our sable allies—were getting into continual trouble; now hitched up helplessly by a lawyer vine, whose sharp prickles, like inverted fish-hooks, rent the skin; now crawling unsuspiciously against a tree-ants' nest, an indiscretion that the fierce little insects visited with immediate and most painful punishment; or else, becoming aware, by unmistakable symptoms, that we were trying to force a passage through a stinging tree-shrub. Whenever we thus came to grief, Lizzie would stop, turn round, and wave her arms about like a semaphore, indicative of impatience, contempt mingled with pity and warning.

Luckily for us, the belt of scrub was not of great extent; Lizzie had already reached its edge, and was peering cautiously through, and we were struggling along, each after his own fashion, when bang went a carbine, the bullet of which we distinctly heard whistle over our heads, and turning round we got a glimpse of Jack, the rough-rider, hung up in a vine, one of whose tendrils had fired off his weapon; and had just time to hear him exclaim, "If I'd only been mounted, this wouldn't have happened," before we broke cover, and all further concealment being now unnecessary, rushed recklessly on to the encampment.

But we were too late to capture any of the men, for I need hardly tell the reader that never had we intended to make use of the curt arguments that Lizzie had relied upon for cutting off the abrupt exit of her quondam friends; it would be quite time enough to commence a system of reprisals when it was ascertained that the blacks had actually been guilty of any atrocity. At present it was mere surmise on our part, and putting altogether on one side the natural reluctance to shed blood, an aggressive policy would have been an unwise one, engendering, as it infallibly would, a bad feeling against any other luckless mariners whom the winds and the waves might in time to come cast upon the inhospitable shores of Hinchinbrook Island.

The sudden report of Jack's carbine, which occasioned a momentary halt, and the few seconds required to burst through the scrub, afforded sufficient time for the male portion of the encampment to make their escape at speed, in different directions, some taking to the water, where they were picked up by the fishermen in the canoes; others diving into the nearest cover, and being lost to sight without hope of recovery. The women and children followed the tactics usual on such occasions, and flung themselves into a heap, similar in colour and contour to that described in a previous chapter, when we searched the Herbert River. The same thing took place again exactly; we sat down in a circle round them, waiting for the deafening "yabbering" to die away, which "yabbering" burst forth in all its pristine discord, whenever one of the party made the slightest movement. Time and patience, however, had the desired effect, restoring tone to their not over sensitive systems, and at the expiration of half an hour, we could distinguish sharp, bead-like black eyes peering at us out of the mass, which had now sunk into silence, but burst out again louder than ever, when Lizzie made her appearance from one of the gunyahs—perhaps the paternal roof, who knows?—where she had retired, swelling with indignation, and as sulky as a whole team of mules. Finding that no one took any notice of her, and half an hour's reflection having, I suppose, convinced her, that if she wanted to make a display before her relations, now was the time, her ladyship came slowly up to the circle, and commenced an attack on poor Dunmore, as she knew him best. To transcribe her words would be impossible, for she put in a native sentence whenever she found herself at a loss for an English one, but the burden of her plaint was this:—

"Plenty d—d fooly fellow, white fellow"—a string of Hinchinbrook vernacular—"Baal you been shoot 'em like 'it dingo"—more Hinchinbrook, but evidently, from the accompanying gestures, indicative of intense disgust—"Baal mine take any more along of black fellow camp"—half sobs—"Baal mine care suppose you fellow all go like 'it—"

And she summarily consigned us to the bottomless pit, as the only place at all suited for such stupid idiots who could refrain from shooting blacks when so grand an opportunity presented itself. Her eyes flashed fire as she delivered herself of her woes, and at the concluding sentence she stamped her little foot, and flinging a short waddy she held, with remarkable dexterity and no mean force, into the midst of the sable mass, she turned round to depart with the dignity of a tragedy queen, when Dunmore jumped up, caught her, and holding her wrist, walked off a little way from us.

"You like 'it one fine fellow red shirt, Lizzie? Mine give you one with 'plenty long tail'. Baal any other gin along of camp have shirt like 'it you; and when piccaninny sit down" (for there was a prospect of her presenting Ferdinand with a little pledge of affection), "mine give that fellow two budgeree flour-bag shirts, suppose only you good fellow girl Lizzie."

Evidently, Dunmore knew the way to the young lady's heart—we nicknamed him "Faust" afterwards—for at the mention of the red shirt, with the lengthy tails, her eyes lost their fierceness, and the allusion to the piccaninny completed his victory, and changing at once from one extreme to the other, as only a black or a child can, Miss Lizzie took her seat in the circle, lighted her pipe, commenced nodding to, and chatting most affably with, her relatives, and looking so kind, that it seemed impossible to believe that an intense longing for bloodshed and cruelty had so shortly before lurked in the breast of the pretty, smiling little savage who was now beside us.

During the task of pacifying Lizzie, the "heap" had again sunk into comparative silence, and only a confused murmur was audible from its depths. Allowing no time to be lost, Dunmore said to Lizzie—who was puffing out huge mouthfuls of smoke, greatly to the astonishment of the other gins, who looked as if they expected to see her suddenly blaze up—

"Lizzie, you ask, suppose they been see any white fellow on island? White fellow in plenty big canoe. That fellow canoe been come like 'it shore. You tell them, 'Baal white fellow hurt you, suppose you been show, where brother belonging to him sit down.' You tell them that, Lizzie."

Lizzie proceeded with the greatest gravity, and evidently with an overwhelming sense of self-importance, to put the required questions, whilst we anxiously awaited her replies.

"Well, what they been say?" exclaimed Dunmore at last, when there was a momentary break in the conversation.

I should imagine that the vernacular of the Hinchinbrook Islanders was not pre-eminently adapted for the noble intricacies of diplomatic intrigue. In the first place it contains but few words, and none representing any number higher than five, so that even the courtly nobleman now presiding over Foreign Affairs, would find the smooth flow of his amenities subjected to rude shocks; and as for expressing any large number either in words or figures—say, for instance, the Alabama indemnity of three millions—to do so, would tax to the utmost the genius of the late Chancellor of the Exchequer. Lizzie, in her first flash of pride, as representing a plenipotentiary armed with extraordinary powers, had commenced negotiations with the dignity and slowness of speech adapted to so exalted a personage. But the shrill chorus which emanated from the audience was decidedly antagonistic to grave deliberation, and the anxious curiosity of the woman superseding the self imposed role of the diplomatist, our envoy lost the pompous tone she had first adopted, and a volley of queries and replies was exchanged so rapidly, and with such appalling shrillness, that we onlookers ran a great risk of being either deafened, or driven out of our senses. At the first slackening of the wordy warfare, Dunmore put his questions, and then Lizzie said—

"Baal there been any white fellow along of here."

"You been sure, Lizzie, ask suppose they been see any big fellow canoe."

Again the same hideous noise now took place, but I will not tire my readers with too minute a description of a scene with which they must now be pretty conversant, suffice it to say, that what with the real or pretended stupidity of the gins, and the imperfect English of our interpreter, we were more puzzled at the conclusion of the debate than we had been at its commencement.

"Had they seen a vessel?"

"Oh yes, big fellow, with wings like 'it bird."

"How long ago?"

"Plenty long time ago."

"One moon ago?"

"Yes, one moon ago."

"Sure it was one moon?"

"No, thought it must be one day ago, and plenty smoke sit down along of big canoe."

Altogether the skein was too tangled for us to attempt to unravel it. They had seen vessels evidently, both sailing ships and steamers, but whether it was yesterday, or ten years back, there were no means of ascertaining; but to make certain that we were not being deceived, we instituted a strict overhaul of the gunyahs, in hopes of finding something that might give us a clue to the fate of the missing men. When we broke up our circle for this purpose, the component parts of the "heap" assumed an upright posture, and it was remarkable to witness the awe with which they regarded Lizzie. At first they seemed afraid to approach her, and stood some five yards distant, watching her whilst she puffed out the smoke from her relighted pipe, and posed herself in an attitude of becoming superiority, for she saw clearly enough that the happy moment for making an impression had arrived. Gradually they drew closer and closer, and at last, three of the eldest gins going down on all fours, crept slowly up until close in front of her, when they stopped, and buried their withered old faces in the sand at her feet. After enjoying their humiliation for a few seconds, she condescended to speak to them, and very shortly they were all chattering away on the most amicable terms.

Meanwhile the gunyahs or native huts, and the camp, had been thoroughly searched, but without bringing to light anything European, except a few bottles, and a pint pot which had been accidentally left behind by one of the party on the occasion of Lizzie's abduction. The gunyahs were better constructed than usual, and consisted of saplings bent in an arch and covered with tea-tree bark, a great improvement on all the native dwellings we had hitherto seen, which were generally little better than a rude screen against the wind. But our time was precious, for we carried but little provision; and we could not afford to loiter about, even in so pleasant a spot as this little bay; so, after dispatching a hasty dinner, we started off afresh, to the immense relief of the gins, and got out of the valley by another pass, which Lizzie showed us. I must not forget to mention one ludicrous circumstance, which convulsed us with laughter. The gins showed such curiosity about Lizzie's pipe, that she handed it round and made them each take a puff. Their expressions, when the pungent smoke caused them either to sneeze, cough, or choke, were most laughable; and I have no doubt that it is still a matter of wonder to them, and a fruitful source of debate over the camp-fires, what pleasure the white man can find in filling his mouth with smoke, apparently with no better object than to puff it out again as soon as possible. Our course now lay due south, and the travelling was much the same as in the morning, that is to say, as bad and as fatiguing as it well could be. Lizzie said she could take us to another bay, where there were sure to be more blacks; and so we trudged patiently along under her guidance, with the sun blazing down so fiercely that the carbine-barrels became quite heated. Our new path was very similar to the last one, seeming to come to an abrupt ter-mination, but really shooting off at an angle, and leading down to a bay, which opened out to our view about five o'clock, and did not present nearly so pretty an appearance as the one we had just left, for the ground seemed swampy, and the beach was a nasty muddy mangrove-flat. We were also disappointed in not finding any blacks; but as there is nothing so bad that it has not some redeeming quality, so this dreary-looking swamp had its advantages, for the trees were loaded with Torres Straits' pigeons, and sea-crabs were abundant. This would enable us to lay in an extra day's provisions, and to extend our search, if necessary, before visiting the 'Daylight', from which vessel we were now separated by more than twenty miles of unknown country, inclusive of a mountainous range. We determined not to shoot any pigeons that night, for they would only keep the less time; and having lit our fire by the side of a small creek, we had supper, and were soon sleeping the sleep of the wea-ry, the watch having instructions to call us at an early hour for the purpose of replenishing our larder before the birds took their depar-ture for the mainland.

A pint pot of tea swallowed—what a blessing it is that this glori-ous beverage is so portable that abundance can always be carried— three of us sallied forth with our carbines, from which we had ex-tracted the bullets and substituted shot, each taking a different di-rection, the troopers guaranteeing a crab breakfast, and Lizzie cut-ting and peeling wooden skewers to roast the game on; for in this climate nothing will keep beyond a few hours, unless partially cooked. I struck away towards the left with the intention of making the mangroves as soon as possible, where I knew I should find plenty of birds. The walk of the day previous had made me a little stiff; but I felt lightly clad, without the heavy blanket, which I had left in camp; and, by way of getting rid of the stiffness, I started off at a run and soon reached my destination, where I sat down until there was sufficient daylight to enable me to see the game. As I rested on the root of a tree, perfectly motionless, I saw something large moving among the mangroves; but the dawn was as yet so uncertain that I could not distinguish whether it was a human being or not.

"If that is a black fellow," I thought, "he's worth all the pigeons put together, and I'll wait quietly to try and capture him," for the object I saw was moving in the direction my companions had taken; and if it were a native, he would be certain to return by the road he had come, when he heard the firing. Sitting still, waiting for anything or anybody, when waited on yourself by hungry mosquitoes, may be agreeable enough to Mr. Fenimore Cooper's typical Red Indian, but I can safely say that it is anything but pleasant work to a thin-skinned Englishman. Daylight had now fully come, and I was beginning to hesitate as to whether I had not better bag some of the birds that were fluttering over my head, and get out of the swamp as fast as I could, when I heard the distant report of a gun, and said to myself, "Well, I'll give the nondescript five minutes more, and if it doesn't turn up by then, I'll blaze away at the pigeons." Half the allotted time had barely elapsed, when another report broke the stillness of the morning, and immediately afterwards I heard a rustling among the mangrove-leaves, and a slight crackling, as though some heavy weight were passing over the arched roots. I stayed quiet, almost breathless, as the noise came nearer and nearer, and, turning my head, I peered through the bush behind which I had taken up my quarters, and saw a fine-looking black gliding cautiously from one to another of the interlaced mangroves. He was evidently quite unsuspicious of any danger in front, and kept all his faculties concentrated on the direction in which he had heard the carbine-shots, which now followed each other rapidly, as the two gunners fired at the birds as fast as they could load.

"Now," thought I, "if I can only cut you off so as to keep you between me and them, I am pretty certain to capture you, my friend;" and, judging my time, I rushed from behind my bush, and was within ten yards of him before he saw me. In his amazement he dropped the long fish-spear with which he was armed, stood one moment undetermined, and then made his way, with the greatest agility, from tree to tree, not back towards my friends, as I had fondly hoped, but straight for the bay. I followed as fast as I could, but he went two paces to my one. I confess I felt sorely tempted to handicap him with a charge of small shot, lodged somewhere about the calves of those lean legs that were carrying him over the roots with such provoking rapidity, and have often wondered since why I refrained; but I did, and continued to scuttle after him, now slipping down and barking my shins, now nearly losing my carbine, and often compelled to sprawl on all fours. He was now forty or fifty yards ahead of me, and I was nearly giving up the useless chase, when an unforeseen accident turned the tables in my favour, and caused me to push on with redoubled vigour. As we approached the bay, the whole of the roots and lower portions of the mangroves became thickly studded with oysters, whose shells, sharp as razors, cut the bare feet of the fugitive; while, on the contrary, they proved of assistance to me by preventing my thick boots from slipping off the treacherous roots. I now gained ground as fast as I had previously lost it, and made certain of capturing my prisoner on arriving at the end of the mangroves, through which I could already catch glimpses of the sea. Animated by the thoughts of bringing a captive into camp, from whom we should probably gain valuable information, I jumped from tree to tree in hot pursuit, and when the bay opened out clearly, I was only a short distance in the rear.

"Now I've got you," I muttered, as the black fellow jumped on to the last stool of roots, and as I was eagerly following, holding my breath for a tussle; when, to my intense mortification, he plunged headlong into the sea, leaving me disconsolate and out of wind, to get back as best I could. I waited until his head reappeared, which was not until he had put a good thirty yards between us, and, pointing my carbine, shouted to him to return or I would fire. It was quite useless. He went quietly out seaward, and at the last, when I turned unwillingly to retrace my steps, I saw his black head bobbing about on the calm surface. When, after a series of involuntary feats on the mangrove rope, I again stood on 'terra firma', all the pigeons had left; and I was compelled to make my way back to camp, empty-handed, muddy, cut about the shins, and with my boots almost in tatters. "So much," thought I, "for trying to catch a black fellow single-handed."

My companions had shot plenty of pigeons, after roasting which we started for the interior of the island, and without meeting with anything beyond the ordinary routine of bad bush and mountain travelling; certainly encountering nothing that would justify me in inflicting a prolix description upon the reader — we arrived late on the following evening at the rendezvous, found the 'Daylight' safely at anchor, and thus completed one portion of our search, without having obtained the faintest clue to an elucidation of the mystery of the 'Eva'.

The pilot reported that, to the best of his belief, no blacks had succeeded in making their escape to the mainland; several canoes had attempted to cross, but they had been seen and intercepted, though none of their occupants had been captured. One canoe he had taken possession of, and now showed us, which was, I think, the most primitive piece of naval architecture any of us had seen. Canoe it could hardly be called, for it was only a sheet of bark curled up by the action of fire; the bow and stern formed by folding the extremities, and passing a tree-nail, or, rather, a large skewer, through the plaits. When placed in the water, the portion amidships, which represented the gunwale, was not four inches above the surface, and so frail that no European could have got into it without a capsize, though the black fellows are so naturally endued with the laws of equilibrium that they can stand upright in these tiny craft, and even spear and haul on board large fish.

We slept in the hold of the 'Daylight' that night, after making all arrangements for a start at early dawn. We trusted that the Cleveland Bay party would have performed their portion of the task, and thoroughly overhauled the southern part of the island, and fully expected to fall in with them on the following day.

Our road lay through most abominable country — stony, precipitous, and in places covered with dense vegetation. The traces of blacks were abundant, and we could travel but a short distance without falling in with some of the numerous camping-places. In many of these, the fires were still smouldering, but the inhabitants had cleared out, most probably warned by those whom the whale-boat had intercepted. Each camp was subjected to a rigid scrutiny, but without revealing anything European, except fragments of bottles, to which we attached no importance, for they were probably flung over-board by some passing vessel, and carried ashore by the tide. These are highly valued by the blacks, who do not use them for carrying water, but break them, and scrape down their spears with the fragments.

To make a spear must be a work of many weeks' duration, when the imperfect implements at the natives' disposal are taken into consideration. In the first place, his missile must be perfectly straight, and of the hardest wood; and no bough, however large, would fulfil these requirements, so it must be cut out bodily from the stem of an iron-bark tree, and the nearer the heart he can manage to get, the better will be his weapon. His sole tool with which to attack a giant iron-bark is a miserable tomahawk, or hatchet, made of stone, but little superior to the rude Celtic flint axe-heads, that may be seen in any antiquarian's collection. These are of a very hard stone, frequently of a greenish hue, and resembling jade; and, having been rubbed smooth, are fitted with a handle on the same principle that a blacksmith in England twists a hazel wand round a cold chisel. The head, and the portion of the handle which embraces it, then receive a plentiful coating of bees'-wax, and the weapon is ready for use. Fancy having to chop out a solid piece of wood, nine feet long, and of considerable depth, from a standing tree, with an instrument such as I have described, which can never, by any possibility be brought to take an edge! I have frequently examined the trees from which spears have been thus excised, and the smallness of the chips testified to the length of the tedious operation; indeed, it would be more correct to say the segment had been bruised out than excised. Having so far achieved his task, there is still a great deal before the black can boast of a complete spear, for the bar is several inches in diameter, and has to be fitted down to less than one inch. Of the use of wedges he knows nothing, so is compelled to work away with the tomahawk, and to call in the aid of fire; and when he has managed to reduce the spear to something approaching its proper size, he gets a lot of oyster-shells, and with them completes the scraping, and puts on the finishing touches. It may easily be imagined what a boon glass must be to the savage, enabling him to do the latter part of the operation in a tithe of the time.

I am afraid that it is often the habit with us Australians to either destroy or carry away as curiosities, the weapons and other little things that the blacks manufacture, utterly regardless of the loss we thus inflict upon them; for without his weapons the wretched native is not only defenceless against neighbouring tribes, who would not scruple to attack him when unarmed, but he is also literally deprived of the means of subsistence. Without his spear, he is unable to transfix the kangaroos and wallabies on which he so much depends for his daily food, and, robbed of his boomerangs and nullah-nullahs, the wild duck can pass him scatheless, and the cockatoo can scream defiance from the lofty trees. I know that this practice of returning laden with native spoil is more frequently the result of thoughtlessness or curiosity than anything else. The implements appear so trumpery, that the European thinks they can be of little use to anybody, but the bad blood thus engendered between the aborigines and the settlers is greater than would be easily credited. Another reason, I would venture to submit, in opposition to this custom is, that in the case of the blacks doing any mischief, no method of punishing them can possibly be devised equal in severity to the destruction of their weapons. A tribe is rendered more helpless and more innocuous by this than by shooting down half the males, and I am sure that if they once found that only in case of mischief was this punishment resorted to, we should hear infinitely less of cattle-spearing and shepherd-murdering than at present obtains. I mention this, not from any good-will towards the blacks, who have been causes of much sorrow to me and mine, but because I am sure that a discontinuance of this idle habit would tend to lessen the existing causes of friction between the two races.

In one of the camps we found a blanket—not, O reader, made of the finest wool, deftly woven at the looms of Witney, but a blanket of Dame Nature's own contrivance, stripped by the aboriginal from the bark of the Australian tea-tree ('Melaleuca squarrosa'), no small shrub, but a noble fellow standing from 150 to 200 feet high, and generally found in the neighbourhood of fresh water, or in the beds of creeks. The bark of this tree is of great thickness, and composed of a series of layers, each of which can be easily separated from its neighbours, and, in fact, much resembling a new book, just issued from the hot-press of the binder. From a portion of this—the inner skins, I imagine—the blacks manage to make a flexible, though not over warm, covering for the winter nights, or for the newly-born piccaninnies. The whole of the process I am not acquainted with, but from all I could gather from Lizzie, the bark is stripped in a large sheet at the end of the rainy season, the inner cuticle of several leaves carefully separated from the remainder, and placed in fresh water, weighted with heavy stones to retain it in its position. After the lapse of a certain time, known only to the initiated, it is taken out, hung up to dry, and at a peculiar stage, before all the moisture has evaporated, it is laid on a flat rock, and cautiously beaten with smooth round stones, which operation opens out the web sufficiently to make it quite pliant, after which it is allowed to dry thoroughly, and is then ready for use. These vegetable blankets are very strong, and must be a great protection to the naked savages, but, despite the ease with which they can be obtained, and the small time and labour occupied in their preparation, but few of the gins have them, and none of the men.

We also found several fish-hooks of a most peculiar shape, and made out of a curious material. In shape they were like a circular key-ring, with a segment of exactly one-third cut out. One end was ground sharp, and to the other was attached the line, cleverly spun from the tea-tree bark. Now, of all shapes to drive a Limerick hook-maker to despair, none, one would think, could have been invented better than this, for the odds are certainly ten to one against its penetrating any portion of a fish, even though he should have gorged it. The material of which these quaint hooks are made is tortoise or turtle shell, for both tortoises and turtles abound on this coast, the former frequenting the fresh-water creeks and lagoons, and the latter the sea. Whether they were cut out of the solid, or whether a strip was soaked, bent, and then dried in the sun until it became firmly set in the required shape, I never could ascertain, but most probably the former plan was adopted.

The whole island seemed to teem with game, and had we been able to fire, we should speedily have made a good bag, but this we dared not do, so I made a mental resolve to return at some future time and make amends for this enforced restraint. At nearly every step, we put up some bird or beast strange to European eyes.

I have no doubt it is known to most of my readers that Australia is destitute of 'Ferae' proper, and that elephants, lions, tigers, etc., are unknown. They will also know that the kangaroos are marsupial animals; that is to say, the females have a peculiar pouch for their young, which are born in a far less advanced state than the young of other animals. But perhaps it is not so generally known that, with two or three exceptions, such as the dingo or native dog, the platy-pus, and several species of bats, the 'whole' of the animals on the continent are marsupial. The brains of this species are very small, and they sadly lack intelligence, in which respect they exhibit a wonderful affinity to the aboriginals who live by their capture.

[ILLUSTRATION—GROUP OF KANGAROOS.]

Of kangaroos there are more than thirty different kinds, but the English are now so well acquainted with this curious animal that it needs no description. There are two things about it, however, that I may with propriety here point out—viz., the use of the pouch, and the various ways in which the kangaroo is serviceable to the settler. The average size of the ordinary female kangaroo is about six feet, counting from the nose to the tip of the tail; and, marvellous though it may appear, the young kangaroo, at its birth, is but little over an inch in length, having a vague kind of shape, certainly, but other-wise soft, semi-transparent, and completely helpless. Now the pouch comes into use. The little creature is conveyed there by the mother's lips, and immediately attaches itself to one of the nipples, which are retractile, and capable of being drawn out to a considera-ble length. Thus constantly attached to its parent, it waxes bigger daily. From two to eight months of age it still continues an inhabit-ant of its curious cradle, but now often protrudes its little head to take an observation of the world at large, and to nibble the grass amongst which its mother is feeding. Sometimes it has a little run by itself, but seeks the maternal bosom at the slightest intimation of danger. It quits the pouch for good when it can crop the herbage freely; but even now it will often poke its head into its early home and get a little refreshment on the sly, even though a new-comer may have succeeded to its place.

AN AUSTRALIAN SEARCH PARTY—III.

BY CHARLES H. EDEN.

A FULL-GROWN "paddy melon," a small and beautiful species of kangaroo, bearing the same resemblance to the "boomer" that a Cingalese mouse-deer does to an elk, was once given to me as a pet, and we became great friends. Whenever I went into the room and opened my shirt or coat, the little fellow would bound in and coil himself snugly away for hours, if permitted; thus showing, I think that he still retained a recollection of the snug abode of his childhood. Like most pets, he came to an untimely end—in fact, met with the fate that ultimately befalls all the members of his tribe who are domesticated and allowed to run about the bush huts in Australia. The fireplaces are large recesses in the wall, and on the same level as the floor. Wood only is burnt, and large heaps of glowing ashes accumulate, for the fire never really goes out, by night or day. As long as it is blazing, the pet kangaroo will keep his distance, but when it has sunk down to living coals, his foolish curiosity is sure to impel him, sooner or later, to jump right into the thick of it; and then—and here his want of brains is painfully shown—instead of jumping out again at once, he commences fighting and spurring the burning embers with his hind feet, and, as a natural sequence, is either found half roasted, or so injured that his death is inevitable.

The uses to which the settler puts this animal are many. He has to take the place of the stag when any hunting is going on (as the dingo has to act for the fox); and most remarkably good sport an "old man" or "boomer"—as the full-grown males are called—will afford; and most kangaroo dogs bear witness, by cruel scars, how keen a gash he can inflict with his sharp hind claw when brought to bay. From ten to twelve miles is by no means an unusual run, and when thoroughly exhausted he makes a stand, either with his back against a tree, or in the water. In both of these positions he is no despicable adversary, and will do much damage to a pack of hounds, by grasping them in his short fore arms and ripping them open, if on land; or by seizing and holding them under, if in the water. Instances are on record of a despairing kangaroo dashing through the dogs on the approach of a dismounted hunter, and severely wounding him. The common practice when the animal is brought to bay is to ride up and pistol him. But, however he may be killed, his useful qualities have by no means departed with his breath. His skin, properly cured, will make good door-mats, boots, saddle-cloths, stock-whips, gaiters, and numberless other useful articles. His long and heavy tail is much valued for the soup it yields; and the hams can be cured, and, thus preserved, find many admirers. The hind-quarters of a large "boomer" will run little short of seventy pounds; and, with the tail, form the only parts commonly eaten by Europeans.

The birds that we encountered were of every form and size; pigeons, some coloured like parrots, others diminutive as sparrows, and of the same sombre hue: pheasants, quail, every kind of feathered fowl that could gladden the heart of the sportsman, were found in abundance, and amongst these the scrub turkey and its nest. This latter bird is so little known, that I am tempted to give a short account of it.

The Australian scrub turkey ('Tallegalla Lathami') is common in all the thick jungles in the north of Queensland, and, though smaller than the domestic bird, is sufficiently like it to be easily recognised, having the same wattle, and neck denuded of feathers. The most remarkable feature about this turkey is its nest, which is composed of sand, leaves, and sticks, piled up into a great mound three feet or so in height, and ten or more in diameter. This enormous mass is not the unaided work of one pair, but of a whole colony, and the material is got together by the bird grasping a quantity in its foot, and throwing it behind him; the ground in the immediate vicinity of the mound is thus entirely stripped of every blade of grass, or fallen leaf. In process of time, the heap partially decomposes, and when the female judges that enough heat has been engendered to serve her purpose, she proceeds to lay her eggs. These are enormous when compared with the size of the bird, and are not simply deposited and covered over, but buried at a depth of eighteen or twenty inches, each egg nearly a foot from its neighbour, and standing on end, with the larger half uppermost. Thus they remain until hatched, though how the bird manages to plant them with such dexterity has, I believe, never been ascertained; no one yet having been sufficiently lucky to witness the proceeding. Directly the little birds chip the shell, they run about with the greatest agility, and their capture is exceedingly difficult. A nest with freshly-laid eggs is a glorious find, for several dozen are frequently extracted, and are most delicious eating.

The evening was fast approaching, when we camped for the night by the side of a nice clear water-hole in a sequestered valley, and, after bathing and having tea, we tried our luck at fishing, for these holes are sometimes full of eels. We prospered, and soon had several fine fellows on the bank, from whence they were speedily transferred to the hot ashes, and roasted in their integrity; they were thus spared the skinning, to which, it is averred, custom has habituated them. Ferdinand and Cato were collecting firewood for the night, for, in the position we had selected, we were not afraid of making a good blaze, and we were sitting and lounging round the fire, conjecturing what had become of all the blacks, and how soon we should fall in with the other party, when Lizzie — who had accompanied the troopers — came rushing back, and said: —

"One fellow snake been bit 'em Cato; plenty that fellow go bong (dead) by-and-by, mine believe."

We all jumped up, and sure enough, poor Cato came slowly towards us, looking the ashy-grey colour to which fear turns the black, and followed by Ferdinand, who dragged after him a large black snake, the author of the mischief.

If Australia is exempt from wild beasts, the number of venomous reptiles with which it is cursed make it as dangerous to the traveller as other tropical countries in which ferocious animals abound. Hardly a tree or a shrub can be found that does not contain or conceal some stinging abomination. The whole of these are not, of course, deadly, but a tarantula bite, or a centipede sting, will cripple a strong man for weeks, while a feeble constitution stands a fair chance of succumbing. But of all these pests, none can equal the snakes, which not only swarm, but seem to have no fear of man, selecting dwellings by choice for an abode. These horrible reptiles are of all sizes, from the large carpet snake of twenty feet, to the little rock viper of scarcely half a dozen inches. The great majority of these are venomous, and are of too many different kinds for me to attempt their enumeration here. The most common with us were the brown, black, and whip snakes, and the death-adder, all poisonous; and the carpet-snake, harmless. The brown and black snakes run from two to eight feet in length, frequent the long grass, chiefly in the neighbourhood of swamps, and from the snug way in which they coil up, and their disinclination to move, are highly dangerous. The latter is very handsome, the back of a brilliant black, and the under portion of a sea-shell pink. Their skin is sometimes used by bushmen as a cover to their waistbelts, which are much beautified thereby. The whip-snakes are of all sizes and of all colours; in fact, under this name the colonists include all the slender climbing snakes, so many of which inhabit Australia. In my opinion, these are the worst; for they come boldly into your room in search of warmth, and may be found stowed away in a boot, or under the pillow, or in any place where they are least expected. Last and worst of our venomous snakes comes the death, or deaf, adder, for it is called indiscriminately by both names, and amply justifies either prefix. The hideous reptile is very thick and stumpy in proportion to its length, which rarely exceeds two feet, whilst its circumference may be put down at one-fifth of its total measurement. The tail is terminated by a small curved spike, which is commonly regarded as the sting; but though when touched it doubles up, and strikes with this horn, as well as bites, I do not think the tail does any material damage, but this opinion one would find it difficult to make a bushman credit. I once saw a man take a death-adder up—quite unintentionally, you may be sure—between two shingles, and it immediately struck backwards with both head and tail, the two extremities luckily meeting above his hand. From the sluggish hab-its of this reptile, it is popularly accounted deaf, and it seems quite unalarmed even by the report of a gun. You may walk over it a dozen times, as it lies basking in the sun, usually in the most fre-quented part of the road, and it will take not the slightest notice, but if touched, however gently, it bites at once.

When I first went to Cardwell, I was talking about death-adders, and the naive remark made by one of the inhabitants amused and at the same time rather terrified me, for the perfect knowledge he exhibited of the reptiles showed plainly how common they were there.

"Nasty things," he said, "but Lord, they won't hurt you. Best not try to get one alive into a bottle, though. I tried that little game on, with a pickle-jar and a stick, but I couldn't get him in, and he doubled up and very nearly bit me; his tail just grazed my hand as it was."

I thanked my informant, and assured him from the bottom of my heart, that whenever I 'did' try to coax a death-adder into a bottle, I would benefit by his experience and use the greatest caution.

The eye of this snake is remarkable for its vivid yellow, crossed by a black longitudinal pupil. The colour of the body is a mixture of dull hues, and the abdomen pinkish; the head broad, thick, flattened, and its 'tout ensemble' hideously repulsive. But I am digressing, and leaving poor Cato still uncared for.

The snake, which was a very large one, had been laid hold of by the boy in the imperfect light, and had instantly bitten him in the wrist, on which the punctures of the fangs were plainly visible. A handkerchief was at once tied round the wounded limb, with a small pebble so placed as to compress the brachial artery inside the forearm, and with the iron ramrod from a carbine as a lever, we screwed this rough tourniquet up until the circulation was in great measure cut off. Luckily Dunmore had a pocket-knife with him, for the sheath-knives we carried were but rude instruments for surgery, and with the small blade he slashed the bitten part freely, while Lizzie, applying her lips to the wound, did her best to draw out the subtle venom. Some of us carried flasks, containing various spirits, and the contents of these were at once mixed — brandy, rum, hollands, all indiscriminately — in a quart pot, and tossed off by the sufferer, without the slightest visible effect. Had the spirit taken the smallest hold upon him, we should have felt hope, for if a man suffering from snake-bite can be made intoxicated, he is safe. But the poison neutralised the potent draught, and poor Cato showed no indication of having swallowed anything stronger than water. With the superstition inherent in the blacks, he had made up his mind to die, and his broken English, as he moaned out, "Plenty soon this fellow go bong," was painful in the extreme.

"It's no use," said Dunmore. "I know these fellows better than any of you, and Cato will never recover. I had a boy down on the Mary River, who was knocked down with low fever. Half a pennyweight of quinine would have put him to rights, but he had made up his mind to die, and when once they have done that, all the drugs in a doctor's shop won't do them any good."

Everything we could think of was proposed, but speedily rejected as useless.

"Pour a charge of powder on the wound," said Jack Clarke, "and then fire it, that will take the part out clean enough;" but we agreed that it would be putting the boy to unnecessary pain, for the poison must be already in the system and beyond the reach of local remedy; and the patient had become drowsy, and repeatedly begged to be left alone and allowed to go to sleep.

"We must walk him about," said Dunmore, "it is the only chance, and painful as it is, I must have it done. Remember, I'm responsible for the boy, and no means must be left untried."

I had withdrawn a little from the group, and as I stood some distance off, outside the circle of light thrown by the fire, I could not help thinking what a scene for the painter's brush was here presented. The dark outline of the lofty gums looked black and forbidding as funeral plumes, against the leaden sky. The rugged range starting up in the rear, cast a threatening gloom over the little valley in which we were encamped, and the distant thunder of a falling torrent could, with little effort, be interpreted as a dull voice of warning from the mountain. The fitful glare of the fire, now sinking, now rising as a fresh brand was added, threw a ruddy glare over the actors in this strange scene; showing the hopeless face of the poor patient, the undemonstrative countenances of his sable companions, and the anxious air apparent in the white men, more particularly in Dunmore, as he knelt over his follower, and tried to inspirit a little hope by dwelling on the chances of recovery. The fantastic dresses, and the wildness of the spot, all combined to add a weird aspect to the group; and recalled forcibly to the mind those scenes of Pyrenean robber-life, so faithfully portrayed by the magic pencil of Salvator Rosa.

But drowsiness was fast closing the eyes of poor Cato, and, as the last chance, we compelled him to walk about, despite his piteous prayers for repose. It soon became evident that our labour was thrown away, for he dropped heavily down from between the two men who were supporting him, and no power could induce him to rise. A heavy stertorous sleep overwhelmed him, his breath came gradually slower and slower, and about two hours from the time of the accident, poor Cato passed away, peacefully and without pain.

Can no antidote be discovered for this virulent poison? Empirics are common who profess to cure snake-bites, but I doubt if they ever really succeed. It is beyond all question that in the early days of Australia, and whilst this beautiful continent was held by Great Britain as nothing more than a useful place for the safe custody of her criminal classes, a convict named Underwood discovered a remedy for snake-bite, and in many cases treated it successfully. The story has by no means died out in the colonies, of the good old laws of brutal terrorism, under which, when a bitten man was brought to Underwood, the latter proceeded to apply his remedy, stimulated by the pleasing threat of a severe flogging, should his treatment be of no avail. He appears to have been a man of great firmness of purpose, for he never could be betrayed into divulging his secret, though many unworthy means were resorted to for that end. The utmost that he would acknowledge was that the antidote was common, and that Australians trampled it under-foot every day of their lives. The way he became acquainted with the remedy was by accidentally witnessing a fight between a snake and an iguana. The latter was frequently bitten, and in every case ran to a certain plant and ate it before renewing the contest, in which it was ultimately victorious, leaving the serpent dead upon the plain. Underwood demanded his pardon and liberty as the price of his precious knowledge, and I believe a mixed commission of military men and civilians deliberated on the case at Sydney, and decided not to grant the convict's request. In due time he died, and with him perished his invaluable secret. It is to be presumed the commission knew what they were about, but undoubtedly their adverse decision has been a real misfortune to all those whose lives are passed in a country inhabited by venomous reptiles. We are much indebted to Doctor Fagren for the exhaustive researches he has made into the action of snake-poison and its remedy—the result of which the reader can find in his elaborately got-up volume, entitled "The Thanatophidia of India"—and on looking over the concise directions given by him for immediate use in the event of such an accident, I do not see that we could possibly have done more than we did, considering the limited material we had at our command. Perhaps, had it been a white man, with a strong constitution, he would have pulled through; for the settled conviction that he was doomed, doubtless accelerated the death of the black boy; but the action of the poison is so rapid, that most cases terminate fatally. Two instances I know of, in which the patient recovered. The first was an Irish labourer, who whilst reaping took up a snake, which bit him in the finger. He walked at once to the fence, put his hand on a post, and severed the wounded member with his sickle. Irishman-like, he forgot to move the sound fingers out of the way, and two of them shared the fate of their injured companion. Paddy walked into the nearest township, had his wounds dressed, and felt no inconvenience from the venom. Under the soubriquet of "Three-fingered Tim," this individual may frequently be met with at Sydney, and, for a glass of grog, will be delighted to recount the whole affair, with the richest of Milesian brogues. The second case was that of a woman. She was going from the hut to the fireplace, when she trod on a snake, which bit her just below the joint of the little toe; for, like Coleridge's Christabel—

"Her blue-veined feet unsandall'd were."

She was in a terrible position; her husband, and the other man for whom she acted as hut-keeper, had both gone out with their flocks some hours previously, and there was nobody about but a poor half-witted lad, who hung about the place doing odd jobs. She was a resolute woman, and made up her mind how to act, in far less time than it takes me to set it down on paper. Coo-ehing for the lad, she went into the hut, and came out again with a sharp tomahawk and an axe.

"Take this," she said, handing the latter to the boy, "and strike hard on the back of it when I tell you."

Thus speaking, she placed her foot on a log of wood, adjusted the keen edge of the tomahawk so that when struck it would sever the toe and the portion of the foot containing the bite, and, holding the handle of the tomahawk steady as a rock, with firm determination gave the words —

"Now, Jim, strike!"

It needed three blows from the back of the axe to complete the operation, for the poor lad grew frightened at the sight of the blood; but the undaunted woman encouraged him, nerved him to a fresh trial, and guided the tomahawk as coolly as if she were cutting up a piece of beef, until the shocking task was completed. With Jim's assistance, she then bound up the foot to arrest the bleeding, and, accompanied by him, rode ten miles into the township, and, need I say, in due course recovered.

In these instances the reader will see that the measures taken were both prompt, and such as would require more nerve than is possessed by the ordinary run of mortals. In the above cases, also, the bitten part was capable of being removed; but for a bite on the wrist, had such an extreme measure as immediate dismemberment been performed, the cure would have been as fatal as the disease.

Poor Dunmore was terribly cut up at the premature death of his follower; Lizzie, having smothered her head with fluffy feathers from some cockatoos that had been roasted for supper, employed herself in chanting a most weird kind of dirge over the body, to which she beat a species of accompaniment on the bottom of a pint pot; while Ferdinand, by Dunmore's directions, had set to work to strip a sheet of bark off a tea-tree, to act as a rude coffin. A great difficulty now presented itself, for we had no tools whatever, and how could we dig a grave? In such hard ground, knives would make no impression, and the body must be buried deeply, or it would be rooted up by the dingoes, whose howl we could plainly hear around us, as they bayed at the moon. We spread ourselves out in different directions, in the hope of finding some rift or recess that would answer the purpose, but in the imperfect light, we failed to discover anything, so were compelled to wait for dawn. I do not think any of us slept much. One of our little party suddenly snatched away in so unforeseen a manner, gave us all food for reflection—for which of us knew that the same fate would not befall him to-morrow? When I dropped off into a slumber, it was so light and broken, that I seemed to be conscious of Lizzie, continuing her melancholy drone, and battering monotonously on the tin pannikin, nor was I surprised when in the morning I ascertained that such had really been her occupation all night; for the purpose of keeping the body from harm, she avowed, but, I am inclined to think, much more from fear of sleeping in the neighbourhood of a dead body, for the blacks are dreadfully superstitious, and frightened to death of ghosts.

At daylight we were lucky enough to find a tree that had been blown down in the late hurricane, leaving a hollow where its roots had been torn out of the ground. In this natural grave we laid the poor trooper, wrapped in his bark shell, and, having raised a pile of stones upon the spot, of such dimensions as to preclude the probability of the body being disturbed by dingoes, we went on our way, silent and melancholy.

AN AUSTRALIAN SEARCH PARTY—IV.

BY CHARLES H. EDEN.

OUR next day was a repetition of the last; camps in abundance, but no blacks, and we had as yet seen no signs of the Townsville party. At night we camped by the side of a large creek, and, after supper, were lying down, with the intention of making up for the broken slumbers of the previous night, when Ferdinand, who had moved higher up the stream to get a private eel for himself and his lady, came back and shook Dunmore, saying—

"Many big fellow fire sit down up creek."

We were on our feet in a moment, and, stealing quietly through the bush, soon saw the glare, and on our nearer approach, could make out many recumbent figures round the fire, and one man passing to and fro, on guard.

"By Jove! it's the Cleveland Bay mob," said Dunmore; "we must take care they don't fire into us. Lie down, or get behind trees, all you fellows, and I'll hail them."

"Holloa there!" he cried, when we had all "planted" (in Australian parlance signifying "concealed") ourselves. "Don't fire, we're Cardwellites!"

In a moment the sentry's rifle was at his shoulder, pointed in the direction whence the voice came; but it was my old friend Abiram Hills, ex-mayor of Bowen, a thorough bushman, and possessed of great nerve, whose turn it then happened to be to keep watch over his slumbering companions. As quickly as it had been raised, his rifle fell into the hollow of his arm, and shouting out, "Get up, you fellows, here are the Rockingham Bayers!" he rushed forward, and in a moment was shaking hands with Dunmore, while the sleepers, uncertain whether it was an alarm, stood rubbing their eyes, and handling their carbines so ominously as they peered into the darkness, that we deemed it the best policy to remain under cover until their faculties had grasped the fact that we were not enemies, and as such to be slain incontinently.

It is a startling thing to be hailed suddenly in the silence of the bush, and had a less experienced sentry than Abiram been on guard, he would most likely have fired. We had also before our eyes the case of a party who not long before had gone out to chastise the blacks, and having split into two divisions, opened a brisk fire upon each other when they drew near again, luckily without effect. Some of these warriors we knew to be amongst ourselves, so it behoved us to exercise caution.

Our greeting was most cordial, and we were soon all assembled round the fire—now blazing up with fresh fuel—smoking the pipe of peace, which we moistened with a modicum of grog from the well-filled flasks of the Cleveland Bayers, and comparing notes, previous to making our plans for the morrow. Like ourselves, they had found plenty of camps, but not a living creature in them; and they were as perplexed as we were as to what had become of their occupants. On their way up from Townsville, they had seen smoke-signals thrown up from the mangroves at the mouth of the Herbert River, and these were answered both from the range behind Card-well, and from Hinchinbrook, so it was evident there were blacks on the island, though most likely concealed in some of the hidden valleys, which, from the volcanic nature of the country, were so plentiful, and so difficult to find.

Lizzie was now brought forward, and subjected to a most rigid cross-examination, with which I will not trouble the reader. She said that they must have crossed over to the main-land, for every place had now been searched. We were in despair, when Abiram Hills said—

"Baal bora ground been sit down along of Hinchinbrook, Lizzie?"

A "bora ground" is a particular place to which the blacks are in the habit of resorting at certain seasons of the year, to hold "corroborries" or dances, and also to perform divers mysterious rites on the young people of both sexes attaining the marriageable age. What these solemnities really are, is but little known, and they seem to differ widely in each tribe. In some, the young girls have a couple of front teeth knocked out; in others they lose a joint of the little finger;

and at that time the hideous lumps with which the men embellish their bodies must be raised. These curious ornaments are formed by cutting gashes in the flesh three-quarters of an inch long, and stuffing the wound with mud, which prevents the edges from adhering, and when the skin grows over, leaves a lump like an almond. The number, proximity, and pattern of these adornments are according to the peculiar tastes of the family, and vary considerably, but the breast, back, shoulders, and arms are usually pretty thickly sown, giving the appearance of a number of fresh graves, placed close together in a black soil field.

[ILLUSTRATION — "NATIVE AUSTRALIAN."]

Abiram's question was one of those lucky inspirations that sometimes strike one, changing, as by magic, obscurity into distinctness, and pouring in a flood of light where no ray could be seen before.

"My word!" — cried Lizzie, her whole face lighting up with eagerness and joy — "my word, close up mine been forget. Mine know one fellow bora ground, plenty black fellow sit down there, mine believe. My word, plenty d — d fooly me!"

We could see from the girl's face that we were now on the right scent, and having ascertained that she could take us to the "bora ground" by the following evening, we finished our pipes, and lay down to sleep, thankful for what promised a possible solution of the mystery.

The Cleveland Bay party consisted of seven white men and two black boys, so we now mustered a strong force. Lizzie would hardly allow us time to swallow our breakfast, so impatient was she to be under weigh; and one wretched man, lingering for a moment later than the rest of us, over a slice of beef and damper, found himself the object of general attention, when our little guide stamped her foot, and, trembling with indignation, said —

"Plenty big bingey (belly) that fellow. Baal he been fill 'em like 'it sundown!"

The travelling was worse than ever now; up and down steep ravines in which the tangled scrub grew so thickly that progress was almost impossible, and we were compelled to wade along the bed of the creek; now tripping over a sharp ledge of rock, now floundering up to the waistbelt in a treacherous hole; past the base of a beautiful waterfall, where the action of the torrent had worn a hollow basin in the rock, in which it sparkled, cool, transparent, and prismatic, in the rays of the burning sun, and where the view, so unlike the generality of Australian scenery, was perfectly bewitching; on, through more scrub, through swamps, and over stiff mountains, wet, draggled, moody, and cross, crawling along after the little black figure in front, that held steadily on its way, as though hunger and fatigue were to it things unknown.

At length, about three o'clock in the afternoon, we found ourselves in a sort of natural funnel in the rock, the end of which grew narrower and narrower as it wound about in curious curves.

"Close up now," said Lizzie, "water sit down along of other side; baal black fellow get away."

We halted for a few minutes to get breath, and to steady ourselves, and then, keeping close together, stepped out of the gloomy passage into the broad daylight. It was a beautiful sight. The "bora ground" had been selected in a miniature bay, of about three acres in extent, closed in by perpendicular rocks, and attainable only by boat, or by the passage through which we had just arrived. In this secluded spot a quantity of coca-nut palms were growing, waifs, carried there by the ocean from the distant South Sea Islands, fructifying and multiplying on the hospitable shore, and shielded from the tomahawk of the native, on account of the shelter they afforded his mysterious retreat. Under the palms stood several conical huts, or lodges, of considerable dimensions, used, I presume, on state occasions for the deliberations of the elder warriors. But the thing most pleasing to our eyes, was the sight of some two hundred natives, of both sexes, and all ages, who now started to their feet, with wild cries of alarm, and motions expressive of the utmost terror, at this sudden invasion of their retreat by the dreaded white man.

Some of the blacks flew to arms at once, and stood with poised spears in a menacing attitude, whilst the gins and piccaninnies cowered together on the beach. We had our carbines in hand, cocked, and prepared to defend ourselves in the event of hostilities, which we earnestly hoped to avoid. Lizzie, who had at last begun to understand that slaughter was not our object, and who had been reconciled to our tame proceedings by the promise of much finery, now advanced towards the threatening natives and made a speech in their own language, to the effect that we wished to do them no harm, beyond ascertaining whether there were any whites among them, though, if we found murder had been committed, we should discover the perpetrators, hold them answerable, and punish them. Rewards were offered for any information that would lead to a knowledge of the real fate of the shipwrecked crew, and an exaggerated estimate of our strength, and the capability of our firearms, was given by our interpreter, on her own account, and was perfectly intelligible to us from the signs and gesticulations she made, and the scorn with which she pointed to the rude weapons of her country-men; for the intrepid little girl had marched fearlessly up to the group of warriors.

After delivering her speech, Lizzie withdrew to us, and we waited, rather anxiously, the turn that affairs would take; for a peaceful solution would be far preferable to a fight, in which, though we must ultimately be the victors, yet success would only be achieved at considerable loss of life, probably on both sides.

Whilst matters rested thus, and the blacks were holding an animated discussion, one of the troopers espied a solitary dingo on the rocks overlooking the "bora ground," and distant from us about fifty yards. Lizzie at once said —

"Suppose you shoot 'em that fellow dingo, plenty that frighten black fellow."

"By Jove, Lizzie, what a good idea!" we said. "Who's the best shot; for it will be fatal to miss?"

"Let your boy fire," said Abiram, "it will astonish them much more if they see it done by a black; and let Lizzie warn them of what is going to take place."

"You believe you shoot 'em that fellow dingo?" asked Dunmore of Ferdinand.

"Your (yes), marmy, mine believe."

"Plenty big glass of rum, suppose you shoot 'em bony (dead)," added Abiram.

The trooper's eyes glistened, and he licked his lips as if the spirit were already won.

Meanwhile Lizzie had told her countrymen to watch the dog, and they would see him killed, and the blacks stood straining their eyes at the doomed dingo, who, with pricked ears and drooping tail, stood motionless against the sky-line, intently surveying the unusual scene beneath, and wondering probably how soon he should get the relics of the roasted fish, whose fragrant odour had assailed his nostrils, and drawn him into his present position.

It was a moment of intense suspense while the trooper raised his carbine—slowly and deliberately; no hurry, not even the quiver of a muscle, for his mind was on the rum, and he recked little of the moral influence of a successful shot;—we drew a long breath of relief as the weapon flashed forth, and the dog, making a convulsive bound forward, fell stone dead at the foot of the rocks, where it was instantly surrounded by the awestruck savages, who carefully examined the body, and thrust their fingers into the bullet-hole, for the ball had passed clean through the animal, just behind the shoulder-blade.

The trooper first loaded his empty barrel, and then twitching Abiram by the sleeve, whispered, "You give 'em rum now. Plenty you make him strong, mine believe." His task was accomplished, and that the reward should immediately follow was with him a natural consequence.

Ferdinand's shot and Lizzie's eloquence had, however, rid us of all further trouble. The blacks laid down their arms, and expressed themselves quite willing to assist us in any way. They vehemently denied having seen any white men, but acknowledged that some had been heard of on the Macalister River, and thought they were detained by the tribes inhabiting its banks. They were cognizant of our expedition up the Herbert, and knew that we were searching Hinchinbrook, but never thought we should have found them in their present position.

It was now evident that further search on Hinchinbrook was useless. There was no reason to doubt the truth of what they told us, for Lizzie would have gathered information had there been any outrage, or some small piece of rag or blanket would have betrayed them. That the unfortunate men might be on the Macalister was not improbable, and thither we must bend our steps, as the last resource. If we were unsuccessful then, we could only conclude that the vessel had foundered at sea, and we should have the melancholy satisfaction of knowing that we had done everything in our power to rescue the sufferers.

We camped for the night at one extremity of the little bay, while the natives occupied the other, in which there was a well sunk, where we supplied ourselves with fresh water. We soon became on friendly terms with our wild neighbours, but took care never to linger amongst them singly, and always had our weapons ready for immediate use.

In the evening Lizzie came over from the blacks' camp, where she had been holding a great palaver, and asked us if we should like to see a "corroborrie," or dance; and much pleased at getting a glimpse of the native customs, and glad of anything to break the monotony of our lives, we followed her to the group of palms, and there took up our positions to watch the proceedings. A tremendous fire was soon flaming on the beach, near it the gins and piccaninnies assembled, with bits of stick, clubs, and calabashes, on which to beat time. Some thirty of the men then stood up, armed with spears, tomahawks, nullah-nullahs (war-clubs), and boomerangs, and commenced a series of ludicrous antics, to a most melancholy dirge chanted by the women, a kind of rude time being observed. Gradually, however, they grew excited, and worked themselves up by going through a sort of mock fight; and when at the last the women danced round them with torches, all howling and shrieking at the top of their voices, and banging the calabashes with kangaroo bones or anything that would add to the noise, the whole scene reminded one of the infernal regions broken loose. This lasted an hour, at the end of which time we withdrew, after expressing ourselves highly gratified, and the whole camp was shortly buried in repose. We kept double sentries, but we might all have gone to sleep, for there was no symptom of treachery. At daylight we had breakfast; gave the warriors and gins a few trifling things we could spare, such as knives, two or three blankets—for we hoped to reach the township that night—and, wonder of wonders to the savages, some matches (nearly all of which they expended in verifying the fact that they would go off), and then took our departure from the "bora ground," guided by a native, who showed a very short way, unknown to Lizzie, by which we arrived at the 'Daylight' early in the afternoon, to find that the latter had been joined by the 'Black Prince', the steamer that had brought up the Cleveland Bay party. We quitted in our little craft for Cardwell, and the Townsville men went south in their steamer, intending to get some shooting at the Palm Islands before going home for good. Eleven o'clock that evening saw us at our township, fully determined to carry out the work thoroughly by searching the Macalister River, an account of which I hope to give in a future chapter.

AN AUSTRALIAN SEARCH PARTY—V.

BY CHAS H. EDEN.

HOW WE EXPLORED THE MACALISTER RIVER.

The reader who has been good enough to follow me so far, will see that hitherto our efforts had been unattended with the slightest success, and that the fate of the missing schooner and her living freight still remained buried in the deepest mystery. To say that we were not disheartened by our numerous disappointments would be untrue, for we well knew that each closing day rendered our chances of affording relief to the survivors more and more difficult; so much so, in fact, that at the council assembled to discuss the matter in the large dining-room of the hotel, several voices urged the expediency of abandoning any further attempts. Much valuable time, they remarked, had been already expended by men to whom time represented money, nay more—the means of living. Their own avocations imperiously demanded their presence, and although they were the last men in the world to desert their fellow-beings in extremity, still, in a country where every man lived by the sweat of his own brow, self-interest could not be entirely sacrificed.

[ILLUSTRATION—AUSTRALIANS IN CAMP.]

Even we, who were most anxious to organise another expedition, could not but acknowledge that the searchers had much justice on their side; but when we were discussing matters in rather a despondent tone, a new ally came to the front in the person of Jack Clarke, the horse-breaker.

"Where do you propose going next?" he asked Dunmore.

"We must search the ranges at the back of the township first, and another party must go up the Macalister River," was the reply.

"Need both parties start at the same time?"

"The chances of success would, of course, be greater if they did," replied the officer, "but still it is not absolutely necessary."

"Well," said Jack, "suppose you take the pilot boat, and go up the river, which will take much longer to explore than the ranges; and, at the end of a week, we shall have got our own affairs pretty straight, and will beat all the country at the back, and join you on the Macalister. What do you think of that, mates?" he added, turning to the company. "Won't that suit us all?"

"Capitally!" was echoed from every side, and after sundry drinks the party broke up; Dunmore and I hastening to make immediate preparations for our new trip.

The Macalister River was at this time most imperfectly known; for, lying to the extreme north of Rockingham Bay, its fertile banks had hitherto attracted little or no attention; the great sugar industry being then comparatively in its infancy in Queensland. A dangerous bar at its mouth, over which heavy rollers were always breaking, made pleasure-seekers rather shy of attempting its entry, more particularly as the muddy mangrove flats held out small hope of aught save mosquitoes and blacks. Since then the sugar-cane has become one of the chief sources of wealth to the colony, and, in the search for land adapted to its growth, the Macalister was not likely to remain long in obscurity. Along its beautiful banks were discovered many thousands of acres of magnificent black soil country, without a stick of timber to impede the plough, over which a furrow, miles in length, could have been turned without an inch of deviation being necessary.

Where the wretched bark 'gunyah' of the native stood, is now found the well-finished house of the planter; and where the savage pastimes of the 'bora' ground once obtained, and the smoke from cannibal fires curled slowly upwards to the blue vault of heaven, is heard the cheerful ring of the blacksmith's hammer, the crack of the bullock-whip, as the team moves slowly onward beneath the weight of seven-feet canes, and the measured throb of machinery from the factory, where the crushed plant is yielding up its sweets between the inexorable iron crushers. In this, our newest world, improvements when once set afoot, proceed with marvellous celerity, and a turn of Fortune's wheel may in a single year convert a howling wilderness into a flourishing township. But I find myself digressing again, and resisting rambling thoughts, must revert to our preparations for the morrow.

[Illustrations KANGAROO. and ORNITHORHYNCHUS PARADOXUS.]

The meeting at which we had just been present, took place on the morning following our return from the search on Hinchinbrook Island; and not only was another day indispensable for the arrangements that were necessary, but we also felt that one more night of comfortable rest would render us better able to encounter the fatigues of the coming expedition. Only bushmen and explorers can appreciate the intense enjoyment of a night of unbroken rest between the sheets, after knocking about for a length of time, catching sleep by snatches, and never knowing the luxury of undressing. Turning in like a trooper's horse, "all standing," as the nautical phrase is, may be an expeditious method of courting the sleepy god, but it certainly is not the best for shaking off fatigue. Bound up in the garments you have carried all day, the muscles are unable to relax to their full, the circulation of the blood is impeded, and your slumber, though deep, is not refreshing; more particularly when— as had happened to us on this last trip—our boots were so soaked that we were afraid to take them off, lest we should find it impossible to struggle into them in the morning. Dunmore's camp was also some distance from the township, and he had to visit it to find out how matters had gone on in his absence, to get another trooper in the place of poor Cato, and to replenish his exhausted wardrobe and ammunition.

But I will not occupy the reader with all these minor details, nor with the numberless little trifles that it devolves upon the leader of such an expedition to remember, suffice it to say that by noon on the following day, all our preparations were completed, and we shoved off from the beach in high spirits, the party consisting this time of nine, viz., Dunmore, the pilot, two boatmen, Lizzie, three troopers, and myself, about as many as the boat could carry comfortably. A rendezvous had been arranged on a known portion of the river; the other expedition was to start in seven days; and, according to our programme, if all went well, we should meet on the tenth, or on the eleventh day at furthest.

The sea-breeze was blowing steadily, cresting the tiny waves which sparkled in the hot sun as they broke into foam, and under its grateful coolness we glided comfortably along, with a flowing sheet. The bar at the mouth of the Macalister was eighteen miles distant, and we hoped to cross it about sunset, when the breeze would have dropped, and the passage through the surf would be readily distinguishable; but our plans were completely upset by one of the troopers espying smoke issuing from the scrub on a small creek, that entered the bay about half-way between the town and the Macalister.

"We had better have a look in here," said Dunmore, "there is no knowing where we may stumble on some information."

Accordingly, the helm was put up, and we ran into the mouth of the inlet, with the wind right aft. Beaching the boat on the soft sand, we sprang out, and advanced cautiously in the direction of the smoke, but, after several minutes of scrambling, we reached the fire only to find it deserted, its original proprietors having seen our sudden alteration of course, and sought the safety of the dense bush, where further search would have been useless.

"Now that we are on shore," said Dunmore, "let us make a billy full of tea; it won't take long. Here, you boys, get 'em like 'it waddy to make 'em fire."

The troopers and Lizzie dispersed in quest of fuel; Ferdinand walking up the bank of the creek, where he was soon lost to sight. A loud coo-eh from that direction soon brought us to the spot from whence it issued, and we found the boy staring at several pieces of timber sticking out of the sand.

"Big fellow canoe been sit down here," he said, on our approach, and examining the protruding stumps, we soon saw enough to convince us that the boy was right, and that we were in the presence of a vessel, wrecked, or abandoned, Heaven only knows how many years ago. With our hands, with pint pots, with a spade we had brought with us—mindful of the difficulty we had experienced in finding a resting-place for poor Cato—with every utensil, in fact, that ingenuity could devise, we set to work clearing away the sand that had accumulated round the old ribs. Suddenly, the tin rim of one of the pots gave back a ringing sound, as if it had struck against metal, and in less than a minute, a much rusted cannon-shot was exposed to view, and passed round from hand to hand. It was of small size, weighing, perhaps, five pounds, though its dimensions were evidently much decreased by the wasting action of damp.

"By Jove!" said Dunmore, "perhaps she was a Spanish galleon, and we shall come across her treasure. Won't that be a find, eh, old fellow?"

"She's more likely a pirate," I answered, as visions of the old buccaneers floated through my brain; and Edgar Poe's fanciful story of the "Gold Beetle" occurring to me, I sung out, "Whatever you do, keep any parchment you stumble across," and abandoned myself to thoughts of untold wealth, whilst I wielded a quart pot with the energy born of mental excitement.

"My word! that been big fellow sit down like 'it here," cried Ferdinand, who, lying on one side, had his bare arm buried at full length in the sand. "I feel him, Marmy, plenty cold."

We rushed to the boy's assistance, and speedily scraped away the shingle, until an old-fashioned gun was exposed to view; it was coated and scaly with rust to such an extent, that we were unable to form any idea as to its age or nationality. It would most probably have been a twelve or eighteen-pounder howitzer, for it was about four feet in length, and disproportionately large in girth; but one of the trunnions, and the button at the breech, were broken off, the portion that had lain undermost had entirely disappeared, and the remainder was so honeycombed, that beyond ascertaining that it was a piece of ordnance, we could elicit nothing from this curious relic of a bygone generation.

Further search brought to light several more round-shot, but in the same state as the first, and we noticed that in several places the timbers were burnt, most probably by the natives, or the crew themselves, for the sake of the copper bolts.

What a number of melancholy recollections are awakened by the discovery of a forgotten memorial of the past, such as this nameless wreck; and if those old timbers could have spoken, what a strange record of hopes unfulfilled, and high adventure unachieved, would have been disinterred from the dark storehouse of the past! That the vessel came in her present position by accident, could hardly be supposed. More probably, having struck on the Barrier Reef, or on some of the hidden coral shelves with which this sea abounds, she had been taken into this secluded creek for repairs. Cook, the great circumnavigator, careened his ship at a spot not far distant from this; but we were unanimously of opinion that this vessel must have become embedded long prior to his time. Not only was the frame-work some distance from the present bed of the creek, but it was raised considerably above the water level. That the eastern coast of Australia is slowly rising from the waves is well known, for in the neighbourhood of Brisbane valuable reclamations have been made within the memory of living men; but at least two centuries must have elapsed to account for the altitude attained by this old craft. Our regret was great at getting no more certain information, but although we persevered in digging until sundown, no casket of jewels, no bags of specie, and no mysterious parchments rewarded us; and with the darkness we were compelled to abandon our search, rather angry at having wasted several valuable hours to such little purpose.

As it would have been madness attempting to cross the bar before daylight, we hauled the boat up on the beach, and made ourselves comfortable for the night. About one o'clock, the trooper who was on watch, awakened us with the news that there was a light out at sea. We thought at first it could only be some blacks in their canoes, spearing fish by torchlight, but it gradually drew nearer and nearer, until at last we could distinguish the distant sound of voices, and the faint rattle of the iron cable as it flew out through the hawse-hole.

"Some coasting craft, I suppose," said Dunmore.

"Most probably, but we shall find out in the morning;" and we were soon again in the land of dreams.

Before daylight we had finished breakfast, and by the time the sun rose, were in the whale-boat, pulling towards the new arrival. She was a dirty, weather-beaten, nondescript-looking little craft, half fore and aft schooner, half dandy-rigged cutter, and the look-out on board was evidently not very vigilant, for we had almost arrived alongside, before a black head showed over the gunwale, and, frightened at seeing a boat-load of armed men in such an unexpected spot, poured out a flood of shrieking jargon that would have aroused the Seven Sleepers, and which speedily awoke from their slumbers the remainder of the crew. There seemed to be only two white men, one of whom introduced himself as the captain, and asked us, in French, to come on board. The vessel was the 'Gabrielle d'Estonville', of New Caledonia, commanded by Captain Jean Labonne, and had put into Rockingham Bay for water, during a 'beche-de-mer' expedition. Anything to equal the filth of the fair 'Gabrielle', I never saw. Her crew consisted of another Frenchman besides the captain, and of seven or eight Kanakas, two of whom had their wives on board. As perhaps this extraordinary trade is but little known to the reader who has not resided in China, I will briefly narrate how it is carried out.

From the neighbourhood of Torres Straits to about the Tropic of Capricorn, extends, at a distance of fifty to a hundred miles from the shore, an enormous bed of coral, named the Barrier Reef. There, untold millions of minute insects are still noiselessly pursuing their toil, and raising fresh structures from the depths of the ocean. Neither is this jagged belt—though deadly to the rash mariner—without its uses. In the first place, a clear channel is always found between it and the mainland, in which no sea of any formidable dimensions can ever rise, and now that modern surveys have accurately indicated where danger is to be found, this quiet channel is of the greatest use to the vessels frequenting that portion of the ocean, for they avoid the whole swell of the broad Pacific, which now thunders against and breaks harmlessly on the huge coral wall, instead of wasting its fury on the coast itself. In the second place on the Barrier Reef is found the 'Holothuria', from which the 'beche-de-mer' is prepared. It is a kind of sea-slug, averaging from one to over two feet in length, and four to ten inches in girth. In appearance, these sea-cucumbers are more repulsive, looking like flabby black or green sausages, and squirting out a stream of salt water when pressed. But despite their disgusting appearance, they are a most valuable cargo, from the high price they fetch in the Chinese market, where they are a much-esteemed delicacy. The vessel that goes in quest of 'beche-de-mer' takes several expert divers—usually Kanakas, or South Sea Islanders—and having arrived at the ground they propose fishing, a sort of head-quarters is established on some convenient island, where vegetables are planted, to stave off the scurvy that would otherwise soon attack the adventurers. This done the little vessel proceeds to the edge of the reef, and begins work in earnest.

The sea-slug is found buried amidst the triturated sand, worn away by the constant play of the waves, and only the experienced and keen-eyed Kanakas can detect its whereabouts, by the fitful waving of the long feathery tentacles surrounding the mouth of the fish, which immerses its body in the sand. The vessel being anchored, her boat is got out, and pulled to the smooth water within the reef, the divers keeping a keen scrutiny on the milk-white floor for any indication of their prey. Suddenly, the man in the bows holds up his hand, as a sign to desist from pulling. He drops quietly into the clear water, and the length of time that elapses before his black head reappears, is enough to make a bystander nervous. Often the diver has to encounter his dread enemy the shark, and if cool and collected, generally comes off victorious in the contest. The South Sea Islanders have a thorough knowledge of the habits of this salt-water pirate, and know that by keeping underneath him, they cannot be touched, and they will fearlessly stab the intruder with their knives, and avail themselves of his momentary departure to regain the boat. I have known one instance of a native jumping into the water to distract the attention of a shark that was swimming guard over his friend, and both escaped unhurt; but still, despite their utmost skill, accidents do often occur. In shallow water the 'beche-de-mer' is caught with a five-pronged instrument, resembling an eel-spear. The animals are split open, boiled, pressed flat, and dried in the sun, and after a sufficient number have been taken, they are carried to the island rendezvous and there smoked with dry wood, which last process converts the slug into genuine 'beche-de-mer', fit for the market, and for the palates of Celestial epicures. I tried to cook some, but after boiling it for a couple of hours in a quart pot, it came out like a dirty piece of indian-rubber, and so tough that no teeth could penetrate it.

Captain Labonne welcomed us very cordially—the sight of a strange face must have been a godsend—and most hospitably asked us to share his breakfast, but as it consisted only of dried fish, which smelt most abominably, we declined, and he was very grateful for a couple of pots of sardines which we gave him out of our slender stock. The 'Gabrielle' was on her way to Cardwell for fresh provisions and water, and after the dangers to be avoided had been pointed out by the pilot, we bade adieu to Jean Labonne and his queer crew, though not before one of our party had succeeded in jotting down the features of a Kanaka diver, his wife and child.

AN AUSTRALIAN SEARCH PARTY—VI.

BY CHARLES H. EDEN.

WE now pulled for the mouth of the Macalister River, and on sighting the bar shortly before eight o'clock, were glad to find but little surf running. On our way we passed several water-snakes, one of which seemed of large size, but we were too distant to form any accurate estimate of its length. It was not altogether without misgivings that we encountered the ridge of sand that extended completely across the entrance of the river. Only one of our party had ever crossed it before, and it was known to be very dangerous. The calm water rolled itself up in smooth walls, which sailed majestically along until the upper portion broke into a line of white, and soon the entire mass rushed onward in a sheet of foam.

The great danger in crossing a bar is, that the helmsman either loses his head and permits the boat to present her broadside to the surf, or that the steering power is not sufficient to keep her head straight. Neither of these misfortunes befell us in entering the Macalister, for, from the hour we had selected, the sea was at its quietest, and we got over without shipping a thimbleful of water. We found a broad expanse studded with dense mangrove flats, and it was with difficulty we ascertained which was the main channel. We pulled on until about noon, by which time the mud swamps had disappeared, and we were fairly in the river, which much resembled the Herbert, of which I have already given a description, except that it was smaller, and that the vegetation was more luxurious. On landing, we lit a fire, and cooked our dinner, consisting of ducks and moor-fowl that we had shot on our way up. I never remember seeing water-fowl in such profusion as here. The ducks and geese were literally in tens of thousands, and the beautifully-plumaged moor-fowl quite blackened the mangrove bushes as we passed.

The scenery was perfectly lovely. Tall palms shot up in every direction; wild bananas spread forth their broad leaves, amidst which were seen the bunches of fruit; and the larger trees—fig, Leichhardt plum, etc.—threw their branches across the river, and there interlacing, formed a leafy canopy such as we imagined was unknown in Australia. Some of the young palms we cut down for the sake of the head, which is very pleasant eating. Stripping off the leaves, you come to a shoot twenty inches or two feet in length, the interior of which consists of a white substance resembling an office ruler in thickness, and which tastes something like a chestnut, but is much more milky and sweet. The fruit of the wild banana has a most delicious flavour, but is so full of small seeds that it is impossible to swallow it. The huge fig trees, with which the banks of most of the northern rivers abound, have the peculiarity that the fruit is found growing on the trunk, and not at the extremity of the smaller boughs. On an enormous stem, and at a distance of only a few feet from its base, are seen bunches of figs, and these, though of smaller size than the European fruit, are very palatable, if they can be selected free from insects. Usually, the ants have been first afield, and have taken up their abode in the very heart of the fig, forming a most undesirable mouthful for the unwary stranger. The wild plums are very good, but to attain perfection, should be buried for some days previous to eating. I trust these details will not prove tedious to my readers, but I know from experience the benefit arising from even a slight knowledge of wild fruits and herbs, which have often quenched thirst and assuaged hunger when other food was wanting, and rendered endurable what would otherwise have been a painful journey.

We camped that night where darkness overtook us, close to a thick scrub which lined the bank of the river, and we paid for our stupidity in not selecting a more open spot, for myriads of mosquitoes put sleep out of the question. The truth was that this belt of scrub had lined the river for several miles past, and we hoped at every turn to come to a break, but night set in whilst we were still between the leafy walls.

Daylight came at last, and we pushed onward. An hour took us into a beautiful black-soil plain of great extent, without a stick of timber, and well watered, not only by the Macalister, which meandered through its centre, but by several large lagoons, overgrown with the lovely white lotus, and crowded with waterfowl. The existence of such a planter's paradise was totally unsuspected, and we all gazed spell-bound on this splendid tract of country, possessing every requisite for successful cultivation, and a water road for the produce. Dunmore was a true prophet when he exclaimed—

"Before a year is past this will be settled upon."

A fine sugar plantation now stands on "Bellenden Plains," with superb cane growing in unwonted luxuriance, and horses and cattle have taken the place of the kangaroos, that we on this first visit found grazing there in troops. In the distance could be seen the coast range behind Cardwell, which seemed to recede inland as it trended towards our position, and sweeping round, approached the sea again farther north, forming a natural boundary to a vast space of available country. A silver line shone out on the mountains, and with our glasses we could make out that it must be a waterfall of very large dimensions. We at once agreed that it must be the source of the very river we were on, the Macalister, but, as the sequel will show, we found so many streams, that most probably we were mistaken in our judgment. We resolved to make this charming spot our head-quarters for the present, as we had everything to be desired— water, game, etc.—close at hand, and, from the absence of timber, no blacks would be able to steal upon us unperceived.

Leaving the pilot and one man in charge of the boat, we trudged along through the high grass, which reached to our middles, and was dripping with moisture from a shower that had fallen during the night; and, after a tedious walk, reached the edge of the scrub. It was thicker than anything we had encountered before, the density of the foliage totally excluding the sun, and giving rise to a dank humid odour that struck a chill to the heart directly you entered. We wound along the path, or rather track, that the blacks had made, with the greatest difficulty. It was all very well for the troopers, who had stripped, but our clothes hitched up on a thorn at every other step. One of our most provoking enemies was the lawyer vine, a kind of rattan enclosed in a rough husk, covered with thousands of crooked prickles. These, with their outer covering, are about an inch and a quarter in diameter, and extend to an enormous distance, running up to the tops of lofty trees, and from thence either descending or pushing onward, or festooning themselves from stem to stem in graceful curves of indescribable beauty. From the joints of the parent shoot are thrown out little slender tendrils, no thicker than a wire, but of great length, and as dangerously armed as their larger relation. These miserable little wretches seem always on the watch to claw hold of something, and if you are unhappy enough to be caught, and attempt to disengage yourself by struggling, fresh tendrils appear always to lurk in ambush, ready to assist their companion, who already holds you in his grasp. I have measured the length of one of these canes, and found it over 250 paces; and this is not the maximum to which they attain, for I have been assured by men employed in cutting a telegraph road through the scrub that they had found some over 300 yards long. They seem to retain the same circumference throughout their whole length, and, as the bushman puts everything to some use, the lawyer is divested of his husk, and takes the place of wire in fencing, being rove through the holes bored in the posts as though they were ropes. It is almost needless to add that this cane derives its 'soubriquet' of "lawyer" from the difficulty experienced in getting free if once caught in its toils.

Another of the torments to which the traveller is subjected in the North Australian scrubs, is the stinging-tree ('Urtica gigas'), which is very abundant, and ranges in size from a large shrub of thirty feet in height to a small plant measuring only a few inches. Its leaf is large and peculiar, from being covered with a short silvery hair, which, when shaken, emits a fine pungent dust, most irritating to the skin and nostrils. If touched, it causes most acute pain, which is felt for months afterwards—a dull gnawing pain, accompanied by a burning sensation, particularly in the shoulder, and under the arm, where small lumps often arise. Even when the sting has quite died away, the unwary bushman is forcibly reminded of his indiscretion each time that the affected part is brought into contact with water. The fruit is of a pink, fleshy colour, hanging in clusters, and looks so inviting that a stranger is irresistibly tempted to pluck it; but seldom more than once, for though the raspberry-like berries are harmless in themselves, some contact with the leaves is almost unavoidable. The blacks are said to eat the fruit; but for this I cannot vouch, though I have tasted one or two at odd times, and found them very pleasant. The worst of this nettle is the tendency it exhibits to shoot up wherever a clearing has been effected. In passing through the dray tracks cut through the scrub, great caution was necessary to avoid the young plants that cropped up even in a few weeks. I have never known a case of its being fatal to human beings; but I have seen people subjected by it to great suffering, notably a scientific gentleman, who plucked off a branch and carried it some distance as a curiosity, wondering the while what was causing the pain and numbness in his arm. Horses I have been die in agony from the sting, the wounded parts becoming paralysed; but strange to say, it does not seem to injure cattle, who dash through scrubs full of it without receiving any damage. This curious anomaly is well known to all bushmen.

For a couple of hours we followed the tortuous windings of the track, without we white men having the faintest conception where we were going, though the troopers and Lizzie declared that we were pushing straight through. At length a ray of sunlight became visible, and in a few minutes we emerged from the sombre depths of the jungle, and found ourselves on the banks of a splendid river, the Mackay. Traces of blacks were seen in every direction, the white sand being covered with their foot-prints. Abandoned gungales were plentiful on the opposite bank, which was clear of scrub, and whilst we were eating the damper and beef with which each of the party was provided, Lizzie espied a thin column of smoke at no great distance.

We approached it as cautiously as possible, taking advantage of every shrub that offered a cover, and finally, lying down and worming our way through the grass on all fours, a mode of progression that is in itself particularly fatiguing and objectionable, but not without excitement, for we never knew the moment when we might chance to put our hands on a dormant snake, or find ourselves sprawling over a nest of bulldog ants. We were successful in completely surprising the camp, which consisted entirely of gins and piccaninnies, all the males, as usual, being out hunting. The gins spoke quite a different language from that of the Hinchinbrook and Herbert River people, and Lizzie was a long time before she could make them understand. They seemed to know nothing of any white men, nor, I may say, of anything else in particular. They were ignorant where the Mackay rose, or where it debouched, and could give us no information regarding the waterfall we saw on the distant range, what river it supplied, or what kind of country was between us and the hills. Altogether they were a most unsatisfactory lot; and having rummaged their camp without finding any suspicious articles, and threatened them with wholesale destruction if they gave warning of our approach to any other tribe, by either smoke signals or messengers, we departed, much disgusted.

On arriving at the edge of a small copse, at a short distance from the camp, we found the arsenal of the male portion of the tribe. Why they had stacked their arms so far away from the gungales we never could make out; but there they were, consisting of the usual spears and shields, and, in addition, several of the enormous swords used by these natives, of which we had often heard, but that few of our party, except Dunmore, had ever seen. These curious weapons are made of the heaviest iron-bark wood, are about five feet in length, by as many inches in breadth, and about an inch thick in the centre—rather more than less, and both edges scraped down to as sharp an edge as the material will receive. They are slightly curved; but the most wonderful part about them is the handle, which is so small that a European can with difficulty squeeze three fingers into it. The mystery is, how do they use them? for Goliath of Gath could never have wielded an instrument as heavy as this with one hand. It is supposed that the warrior raises the cumbrous weapon on his shield, and having got within sword's length of his enemy, lets it drop on his head. This portion of a black's frame is undeniably hard; but such a blow would crush it like an egg-shell; and as he may be credited with sufficient sense to know this, it seems difficult to understand why he should stand still and allow such a disagreeable operation to be performed. Whether or not the use of these weapons has been discovered since I left Australia, I am unable to say; but certainly up to that time we who lived in their neighbourhood were unable to appreciate the varied excellencies they doubtless possess.

We pursued our way up the Mackay River in hopes of finding some termination to the thick scrub on the opposite bank, so that we might return to our boat without having to thread its intricate mazes again; and in this we were successful, finding a break in the jungle an hour before sunset, which at once admitted us to the plain,

through the centre of which ran the Macalister, and in due course
we reached our camp, where, after having a glorious "bogey" (the
Australian term for bathing) in the river, and overhauling each other well, to see that no ticks were adhering to our skins, we had supper, and turned in, having done little good, except finding a road to
the Mackay less tedious than the one we had taken in the morning.
The ticks that I mentioned just now, are little insects no bigger than
a pin's head when they first fasten on to you, but soon become swol-
len with blood until larger than a pea. They do no harm to a man
besides the unpleasant feeling they occasion, but they almost invar-
iably kill a dog. Nearly all our dogs fell victims sooner or later to
either the alligator or the tick.

HOW WE EXPLORED THE MACKAY RIVER.

We now determined to carry with us enough tea, sugar, and flour to last for a week, and to work up towards the unknown country at the head of the Mackay, leaving the boat in its present position, under the charge of two men. We intended to push towards the range whence both the Macalister and the Mackay rivers drew their supply; and as the former stream in its windings over the open plain approached within a mile of its large neighbour, we resolved to move the boat a little further up before starting on our new expedition. By occasionally lightening her, and dragging her over the shallows, this was accomplished in a couple of hours, and we finally halted at a bend in the river where the bank was high enough to shield the boat from all observation, whilst the scrub bordering the Mackay, standing at less than a quarter of a mile distant, the men left behind could easily see if any considerable body of blacks moved between the two streams, and could take the bearings of all smoke arising from fires in the direction of the coast, so that we might visit them hereafter, if deemed necessary. The fact of two rivers, each containing a constant supply of water, being found in such close proximity to each other, caused much remark, for none of us had ever observed a similar instance in Australia, which is as a rule very deficient in permanent rivers.

We now turned our attention to getting sufficient provisions cooked to last the exploring party for three days, as we were determined to employ the utmost vigilance, and show as little smoke as possible, for nothing creates such suspicion amongst the aboriginals as seeing fresh fires constantly lighted, unless accompanied by the smoke signals, which I have described in a former chapter. As we were utterly ignorant of the code they employed, we resolved only to light our fires at night, and not even then unless we found some sequestered spot where the flame would be unseen. Some of us at once started for a large lagoon that we had passed in the morning, and creeping up through the long grass, found its surface quite covered with water-fowl of every description, from the black swan to the beautiful pigmy goose. A volley, fired at a concerted signal, strewed the surface of the lake with the dead and wounded, and we were compelled to stand idly on the bank until the wind wafted the game ashore, for at the report of the guns two or three heavy splashes and as many dusky forms gliding into the water betokened that we had disturbed alligators, either having a nap, or lying in wait for kangaroos and wallaby coming down to drink. More than one house now stands on the margin of this lagoon, but their inhabitants are still afraid to bathe in the broad sheet of water spread so invitingly before them.

Having secured our game, we returned to the boat, and after plucking and splitting open the birds, some were roasted over the fire for immediate use, but by far the greater number were boiled in a pot, which was portion of the boat's furniture when on an expedition. One of the troopers had with a tomahawk stripped off a sheet of bark, and on this was manufactured a gigantic damper. For the information of such of my readers as may be unacquainted with Australia, I must explain that damper is unleavened bread, well kneaded and baked in the ashes. But simple though such a rough form of loaf may seem from the above description, it is in reality a very difficult thing to turn out a thoroughly good damper, and only practice will enable the new-comer to obtain the sleight of hand necessary for the production of a first-rate specimen. In form a damper resembles a flat cheese of two or three inches thick, and from one to two feet in diameter. Great care and much practice are requisite to form this shape so that no cracks shall appear, and when this is done the work is by no means over, for the exact heat of the fire must be judged by the cook, otherwise he will either burn up his dough, or it will come out a crude, sodden, uneatable mass. A good wood fire that has been burning several days, and has gained a quantity of ashes, is the best; but wood is plentiful enough in the bush, and if you only know the right kind to use, you find no difficulty in soon providing yourself with a glorious heap of glowing embers. Scraping away a hole in the centre of the fire a little larger than the disc, you gently drop it in with your hands, strew it over with enough powdery white ash to prevent the embers coming into actual contact with the dough, and then cover the whole with the glowing coals. Only practice can enable the bushman to judge the exact depth of this layer, which, of course, differs in every case, according to the size of the damper. It is left in this fiery bed until small cracks appear on the covering caused by the steam forcing its way out. This is a sign that it is nearly done, confirmation of which is sought by introducing a knife-blade through the ashes, and sounding the crust. If this gives back a hard sound, the damper may be considered cooked, and is then withdrawn, stood carefully 'on its edge'—never forget this—and is ready to eat when cool.

As there was nothing very particular to do that afternoon, we watched the troopers spearing fish, in which they were most skilful. There is in some of the Australian rivers a splendid fish, called the 'Barrimundi', which not only much resembles the salmon in appearance, but, like it, requires running water and access to the sea. Many a time I have vainly tried to lure them from their watery depths, but no bait would tempt them that I could ever hit on, though I have little doubt that a fly or artificial minnow would prove killing. We could see them in the Macalister, lying with their heads pointed up stream, and seemingly motionless but for the slight waving of the tail that retained them in their places. Having cut several slender switches, not thicker than a tobacco-pipe stem, and sharpened one end with a knife, the trooper Ferdinand, who was by far the most expert among his brethren, grasped this apparently inoffensive little weapon between the thumb and middle finger, whilst the blunt end rested against the ball of the forefinger. Stooping down, he approached to within four or five yards of the fish, which were only a few inches from the surface, and suddenly jerking his switch forward, it entered the water almost horizontally, and rarely failed to transfix a 'Barri mundi', which, darting forward, was soon hampered by the weapon catching in the weeds, and became the prey of its sharp-eyed captor, who had never lost sight of it in its endeavour to escape. This fish is excellent eating, and averages from eight to thirty pounds in weight.

As Dunmore and I were strolling along a small lagoon overgrown with water-lilies, he pointed out to me a pretty graceful little bird, about the size of a jack-snipe, but with longer legs, and most extraordinary claws. I am ashamed to say I shot this poor little fellow, to examine him, and found that each toe measured at least three inches from the leg to the extremity of the claw. This is to enable the bird to run along safely over the floating leaves of the lotus, on which plant it seems to get its living. I had never seen one before; and the simple manner in which Nature had adapted it to its peculiar line of life struck me as both curious and beautiful. What this little bird's scientific name is I never heard, but we colonists call it the "Lotus bird."

As there was a remote chance of the party left with the boats coming in contact with the blacks, it was deemed advisable to leave them a trooper, who would more readily recognise their whereabouts than the white men; therefore a boy known by the not euphonious sobriquet of "Killjoy," was selected to remain with the pilot and his two boatmen, and after dividing the big meat damper in five equal portions, the exploring party, consisting of Dunmore, Ferdinand, Larry, Lizzie and myself, struck out for the opening in the scrub on the Mackay river. We descended into the sandy bed, and crossed to the opposite side, which was much more open country, consisting of park-like land, lightly timbered, but the soil not nearly so rich as the fertile plain through which wound the Macalister. It would be tedious to weary my readers with a minute account of our doings each day; enough to say that we passed through new country of every description, crossing from side to side of the Mackay, to cut off its many bends, and that our progress was but slow, the distant ranges seeming hardly nearer on the third day than they were at starting. We were disappointed in not meeting with any blacks, though their traces were plentiful; and we had commenced to fear that the tribe we had surprised five days before had given warning of our approach, when Ferdinand reported smoke a couple of miles on our right. It was about mid-day when this was seen; and having made a hurried meal off the damper, which I may here state answered its purpose admirably, we crept towards the fire with the utmost caution. Our route took us away from the river, and on arriving at the edge of a small belt of scrub, we could make out that the fire was by the side of a water-hole, but the two hundred yards between it and ourselves was so open, that surprising the camp seemed almost impossible. The hour was in our favour, for the blacks were lying about listlessly, resting themselves after the fatigues of procuring the food of which they had just made a meal. They numbered about twenty of both sexes, and were evidently quite unconscious of our proximity. Detaching the two troopers to make a detour, and cut them off from the scrub in that direction, Dunmore, Lizzie, and I remained perfectly motionless for above an hour, and then, judging that the boys must have reached their position, we advanced towards the camp swiftly but silently. We got over a third of the distance before the blacks saw us, and then ensured a general scrimmage. The women and children jumped into the lagoon, and the men, snatching up their weapons, threw a volley of spears with such force and precision that, had we been twenty yards closer, it would have gone hard with both my companions and myself. As it was, the missiles nearly all fell short, seeing which the warriors dropped their arms and took to their heels, running directly for the spot where Ferdinand and Larry lay in ambush. Both Dunmore and myself fired our carbines over the heads of the retreating Myalls (wild blacks), which completed their panic, and one of them, rushing recklessly forward, was captured by the troopers, and brought by them in triumph to the camp, amidst the yells and jabbering of the gins and piccaninnies.

After half an hour or so, seeing that no harm was intended to them, the women came out of the water, and we were very much pleased to find that they readily understood Lizzie. On being ad-dressed by her, the warrior, who had hitherto maintained a sullen and defiant attitude, became conversational, and readily replied to all the questions put to him by Dunmore. Unlike most of the blacks, he appeared to be very little frightened at the situation in which he found himself, and seemed instinctively to know that all danger was past. On being questioned regarding the shipwrecked crew, he denied all knowledge of any vessel having been lost, but said at once that a white man had lived with this tribe for many moons, though he was dead now. This rather astonished us, and we asked if any relics were still in the camp, upon which one of the gins pro-duced an old sheath-knife, worn down nearly to nothing by con-stant sharpening; half a dozen horn buttons, one of them still sewn to a fragment of moleskin; and an empty tin match-box. We asked how long the white man had been dead, and were told that he died three moons before, of fever, and that we could see his grave if we liked, for it was within a day's journey. There was an openness about this tribe, and a frankness in their answers, that made us cer-tain that all we heard was the truth, and as they had evidently be-friended this poor wanderer, we were anxious to repay them in some measure, and strengthen the kindly feelings they felt for the white men, so we told Lizzie to assure them that our visit was only to search for our lost brethren; that we should like to visit the grave, if one of them would guide us; and that in return for their services we would give them a new knife and a tomahawk.

As they were profoundly ignorant of the use of fire-arms, and we wished to impress upon them the irresistible power of the white man, it was agreed that we should ask them to guide us to the nearest place frequented by kangaroos, and pick off two or three of these animals in their presence, if possible. They were very curious to know the meaning of our "lightning sticks," and we repaired, escorted by nearly the whole tribe, to a neighbouring water-hole, where we could remain concealed, and get an easy shot at any game coming down to drink. We were not kept long waiting, for within half an hour a couple of wallabies came hopping leisurely along, and were very cleverly dropped in their tracks, one by Dunmore, the other by Larry. Our hosts were in ecstasies, and seemed very grateful that a similar fate had not befallen some of their number in the morning; but we made Lizzie explain to them clearly that our object was not to hurt our black friends, unless they were wicked — ill-treating white men, or spearing cattle. A couple of noble emus now came stalking slowly towards the water, and, passing within forty yards of our hiding-place, both fell victims to the breechloaders of Dunmore and myself.

This beautiful bird inhabits the open country throughout Australia, where at one time it was very common, but is now rarely seen in the settled districts. However, in the north emus may be found in plenty; and I do not think there is the slightest fear of their becoming extinct, as some writers suggest. All my readers must have seen this bird at the Zoological Gardens, and remarked its likeness to the ostrich, both in form and habits; but the prisoner portrays but poorly the free majestic gait of the wild inhabitant of the plains. The colour of the adult bird is a greyish brown, the feathers are very loose and hairy, whilst the height of a fine male is often nearly seven feet. The usual mode of capturing these birds is to ride them down, using dogs trained for the purpose to pull them to the ground. The dogs should be taught to reserve their attack until the emu is thoroughly tired out, and then to spring upon the neck; but an unwary puppy will bitterly rue his temerity should he come within reach of the powerful legs, which deal kicks fiercely around, and of sufficient power to disable any assailant. The ostrich always kicks forward, in which he differs from the emu, whose blow is delivered sideways and backwards, like a cow. This bird is very good eating, if you know the part to select; the legs proving tough and unpalatable, while the back is nearly as tender as fowl. But to the bushman the most valuable thing about the emu is its oil, which is looked upon as a sovereign remedy for bruises or sprains when rubbed into the affected part either pure or mixed with turpentine. This useful oil is of a light yellow colour, and from its not readily congealing or becoming glutinous, it is in much request for cleaning the locks of fire-arms. It chiefly resides in the skin, but also collects in great quantities near the rump. The usual mode of obtaining it is to pluck out all the feathers, cut the skin into small pieces, and boil them in a common pot; but a still simpler plan, though less productive, is to hang the skin before a fire, and catch the oil as it drips down. A full-sized bird will yield from six to seven quarts. The food of the emu consists of grass and various fruits. It emits a deep drumming sound from its throat, but no other cry, that I ever heard. Its nest is only a shallow hole scraped in the ground, and in this hollow the eggs, which vary in number, are laid. Dr. Bennett remarks that "There is always an odd number, some nests having been discovered with nine, others with eleven, and others again with thirteen." When fresh they are of a beautiful green colour, and are in much request for mounting in silver as drinking cups; but after a little while the colour changes to a dirty brownish green. One peculiarity about the next is, that the parent bird never goes straight up to it, but walks round and round in a narrowing circle, of which the nest is the centre. I once caught seven little emus, only just out of the shell; but shutting them up for the night in an empty room, I was horrified the next morning to find that they had all been killed by rats. The young ones have four broad longitudinal stripes down the back, which disappear as they grow up. The emu is easily domesticated, and on many cattle and sheep stations tame specimens are funning about the paddocks. To my mind they are an intolerable nuisance, always doing some mischief — either frightening the horses, or stealing things from the workmen. I saw one cured of his thievish propensities for a long time. He always loafed about the kitchen when dinner was being served, and if the cook turned his back for a moment, his long neck was thrust through the window, and anything within reach—from an onion to a salt-spoon—disappeared with marvellous celerity. But my friend caught a tartar when he bolted two scalding potatoes, steaming from the pot. He rushed round and round the little paddock, and at last dropped down as if dead, from pain and fatigue. Poor wretch, he must have suffered dreadfully; and I am sure we all pitied him, except the cook, whose patience he had quite worn out.

Out sable allies were gratified beyond measure when we presented them with the game, and a great feast took place that evening. We neglected no opportunity of gaining information about both the shipwrecked crew and the unknown white man, whose grave we were to visit on the following morning. Through Lizzie we questioned different individuals separately, but they all agreed that such an event as the loss of a vessel and the arrival of her crew amongst the blacks, could not possibly have happened without their hearing something of it. From their imperfect knowledge of time, and their difficulty in expressing any number higher than five, we could not form the slightest idea how long the white man had lived among them; but they pointed to the ranges behind the township of Cardwell as indicating the place where he first joined them.

We camped at the opposite end of the water-hole, not thinking it judicious to remain too close to our allies, and kept a strict watch during the night; but we might all have enjoyed a good sleep in perfect safety, for the blacks were far too busy stuffing themselves with emu meat to think of treachery. Before sunrise we started, guided by our late captive and two of his companions. After a tedious walk, we arrived at an open plain, on which the grass was trodden down in every direction, in some places worn quite away by the feet of the natives—for this was the great "bora ground" of the coast tribes, where the mystic ceremonies mentioned in a former chapter took place. Traversing the sacred plain, our thoughts busy in conjecturing the weird scenes that the posts had witnessed, we came to a little creek whose clear stream babbled cheerfully among the rocks, and soon saw a giant fig-tree, which our guides indicated as being the spot we sought. As we approached we perceived a greyish-looking form on a large limb about ten feet from the ground, and a closer inspection revealed to us that it was unmistakably the body of a white man, rolled up in tea-tree bark, and kept in its position by fastenings of split cane. We could not examine the corpse very minutely, for it was too offensive; but from the portions of the face that still remained, and the long blonde locks and red beard, we satisfied ourselves that the poor wanderer was not one of the 'Eva's' crew; indeed, we judged that his death must have taken place some time before the loss of that vessel. We were much pleased to observe the respect with which the natives had treated the remains, and as they think that exposure either on a platform or in a tree is the most honourable way in which a corpse can be disposed of, we left the body as we found it, and returned to the camp, where we passed the night.

Our damper was now at an end, and we had no flour with us, so made up our minds to return to the boat. On talking the matter over, it seemed quite clear that the shipwrecked men had never been thrown on this part of the coast, and that any further exploration would only be lost time. On the following morning we presented the tribe with our knives, and some matches, and taking a friendly leave of them, started for the Macalister, accompanied by two of the warriors. We reached the boat on the sixth day, found the pilot and his party well, and having dismissed the blacks, with the present of a tomahawk and a blanket, we started at once for the place lower down the river, which had been agreed upon with Jack Clark as a rendezvous. When we arrived at this spot on the following day, the horsemen had not turned up, so we amused ourselves as best we could, fishing, shooting, and eating damper thickly plastered over with honey, for Larry had found a "sugar bag."

The way the trooper performed this feat was not a little ingenious. Having noticed several bees about, he caught one, and with a little gum, attached to it a piece of down from a large owl that somebody had shot. Releasing the insect, it flew directly towards its nest, the unaccustomed burden with which it was laden serving not only to make it easily visible, but also impeding its flight sufficiently to admit of the boy following it. The next was at the top of a large blue gum tree, about three feet in diameter, and sending up a smooth column for fifty feet without a branch or twig. Most people would have given up all thoughts of a honey feed for the day; not so Mr. Larry, whose movements we followed with considerable curiosity. Divesting himself of his clothing, he repaired to an adjoining scrub, and with his tomahawk cut out a piece of lawyer cane twenty feet in length. Having stripped this of its husk, he wove it into a hoop round the tree of just sufficient size to admit his body. Slinging his tomahawk and a fishing-line round his neck, he got inside the hoop, and allowing it to rest against the small of his back, he pressed hard against the tree with his knees and feet. This raised him several inches, when with a dexterous jerk he moved the portion of the hoop furthest away from him a good foot up the stem, and thus—somewhat on the same principle that boys climb a chimney, for the hoop represented the chimney—he worked himself upward, and in much less time than I have taken to describe it, was astride on the lowest branch, and chopping vigorously at the hollow which contained the golden store. The use of the fishing-line now became apparent, for we bent on to its end a small tin billy (round can), used for making tea, and by hauling this up and filling it, Larry soon supplied us with honey enough to fill our bucket and the boat's baler. As perhaps my readers may be tempted to wonder why the bees did not attack the naked hide of the robber who was thus rudely despoiling them, I must state that the wild Australian bee is stingless. It is a harmless little insect, not much larger than the common house-fly, and though it produces abundance of honey and wax, it has not been subjected to domestication, and from its diminutive proportions and its habit of building on very high trees, probably never will be. The English bee has been most successfully introduced into Queensland; and many of the farms in the neighbourhood of Brisbane make a good thing out of their honey and wax.

A meeting was held the next day, at which it was agreed that all further search would be useless, and, indeed, I am certain that every possible measure had been attempted for the discovery of the missing men. There seems every reason to think that the ill-fated 'Eva' was sunk in the cyclone. Most likely she went down in deep water, and all on board her were drowned. Such was the supposition that received most favour at the time, and with it we must rest content until the great day when all secrets are revealed.